THE INNOVATIVE MINDSET

5 BEHAVIORS FOR ACCELERATING BREAKTHROUGHS

JOHN SWEENEY AND ELENA IMARETSKA

WILEY

Published by John Wiley & Sons, Inc., Hoboken, New Jersey.
Published simultaneously in Canada.

For general information on our other products and services or for technical support, please contact our Customer Care Department within the United States at (800) 762-2974, outside the United States at (317) 572-3993 or fax (317) 572-4002.

Wiley also publishes its books in a variety of electronic formats. Some content that appears in print may not be available in electronic books. For more information about Wiley products, visit our web site at www.wiley.com.

Library of Congress Cataloging-in-Publication Data is available

ISBN 9781119161288 (Hardcover)
ISBN 9781119161301 (ePdf)
ISBN 9781119161295 (ePub)

Cover Design: Paul McCarthy
Cover image: © Chuwy / GettyImages

Printed in the United States of America

10 9 8 7 6 5 4 3 2 1

John: To Jenni and William and Michael, thanks for showing me what the mindset of discovery looks like each and every day.

Elena: To my amazing parents Rada and Dimitar for helping me discover the world and to my husband Bryan and son Dimitar for inspiring me to be a better person every day.

Contents

Preface

For more than 15 years I have been speaking about, or conducting training sessions on, innovation for leading corporations across the globe. Clients always tell me during initial calls that they are interested in finding ways to increase innovation in their organizations. If I've heard the question once, I've heard it a thousand times: "What can we do to make our company more innovative?"

Individuals who see me speak or people I run into in my day-to-day life often ask me another question. Whether I'm sitting next to someone on an airplane, serving on a committee for a nonprofit organization, or talking with other parents from my children's school, students in our school of improvisation, or audience members at our theater, people always ask me a little bit about my life and what I do. After we chat a bit they want to know: "What are some things I can do to make myself more innovative?"

This book will try to help answer both questions. Like many of you, my life has been mostly a journey. Many of the stops on the journey have been quite unexpected; my successes and failures have been unpredictable at best. I'm a different person than I was 15 years ago. I have learned more than I've taught and I made some plans, most of which changed. I've been working hard to be a good husband, a good father, and a contributing member of my community, to build a business, and to share what I have learned about innovation with the thousands of people I speak to and train each year. This book is a collection of observations, stories, and practical advice about how we can become more innovative at work and at home, the science behind our approach, and conversations with people who are truly living behavioral innovation—mixed in with some comedic levity.

I've written this book in concert with a woman who has played a significant role in the success of every aspect of the Brave New Workshop Creative Outreach, Elena Imaretska. She is an international business MBA turned improviser, performer, and new product developer.

Prior to joining the Brave New Workshop, Elena was raised in Bulgaria, studied in Germany, worked in Japan, and received a BA degree at Colorado College in Colorado and an MBA from Arizona's Thunderbird School of Global Management. It's fair to say she's been through the ringer on three continents and recognizes the value new ideas, diversity, and different points of view can bring to a company. Our philosophies about the mindset of discovery as it relates to innovation are extremely similar. This book is from my point of view, but any time I reference *we*, Elena is right there with me.

Elena and I chose to include interviews with innovative thinkers and doers from diverse fields. You will hear from leaders who spend their days in places ranging from the corporate world to a social enterprise venture to city government to a convent in Minnesota to Martin Luther King's church in Montgomery, Alabama. Their stories are personal and diverse for a reason: Innovation demands that we open our minds to all possibilities as a way to find our own personal path to success and solution. We ask that you hear the messages of these stories and then personalize them in a way that works for you. Their journeys and insights will illustrate the concepts we will introduce you to, and hopefully nudge you a bit closer to believing that you yourself can foster an innovative mindset.

This book's goal is to bring the behavioral side of innovation to the forefront of the conversation. We hope it inspires you to embrace the idea that like an athlete or an artist, you can create a daily, weekly, monthly, yearly, and lifetime plan to practice and improve your personal innovation behaviors. It will show that everyone is capable of life-changing and perhaps world-changing innovation, and that if we all choose to simply spend more time in a mindset of discovery instead of a mindset of fear, our lives and this world can become richer, more productive, and more innovative.

In Chapter 1 we explain how focusing on behavior is an important, and often forgotten, element of creating an innovation culture. Chapter 2 sketches the ups and downs of our organization's growth to illustrate how we have tested the mindset of discovery in our entrepreneurial practice. It also shamelessly attempts to convince you to read on by outlining how an innovative mindset can benefit you personally. Chapter 3 dives into the world of improvisation, and specifically its behavioral and cultural norms, whose study and experience gave us the mindset of discovery. Chapter 4 outlines ways to practice and weave key behaviors into your daily life, and provides examples from the world of improvisation and from a centuries-old spiritual practice. Chapter 5 reveals the mindset of fear and links current research to the reasons behind our quest to transform fear into discovery. After scaring you sufficiently, we deconstruct the mindset of discovery in Chapter 6, and you get to learn why I married my wife. Chapter 7 touches on habit formation and techniques for transforming our behaviors. Chapters 8 through 12 each dive into a specific innovation behavior and give you lots of practical ways to practice that behavior and integrate it into your daily routines. Finally, Chapter 13 wraps it all up together and appeals to your idealism to inspire you to apply the ideas of this book to your daily life.

Acknowledgments

T hank you to Brian Bellmont, Mollie Wulff, and the team at Bellmont Partners, and to Maygen Keller and everyone at the Brave
New Workshop. Without your talents and hard work this book would
not have been possible.

1

Behavioral Innovation: Remembering the Human

Chad
What's up?

Melanie
Not much, working on a brainstorming list.

Chad
For what?

Melanie
Brad said everyone on the team had to come up with 10 new ways our product could be used by 10 new types of customers in 10 new markets.

Chad
Sounds simple enough.

Melanie
Truly.

Chad
Did he give you any guidelines?

Melanie
The usual, think outside the box (ugggh!!), no bad ideas, be disruptive, how would Google or Apple approach the list?

Chad
Did he give any restrictions?

Melanie
The usual, has to match our brand, needs to have a huge ROI, has to be for the demographic of moms ages 26 to 38 with more than $42,000 annual disposable income, needs to pass the legal department test and work within our current distribution, packaging, and marketing plans.

Chad
How's it going?

Melanie
So far, I have a piece of paper and on the top I have written the word "ideas."

Chad
How long have you been working on it?

Melanie
Six hours.

Chad
When did he ask you to do this?

Melanie
41 days ago.

Chad
When is it due?

Melanie
Tomorrow at 10:30 A.M.

Chad
Want to go get coffee?

Melanie
Meet you at the elevator.

W hen people approach our organization—Brave New Workshop Creative Outreach—to work with them on their innovation programs, the first step is always to simply set up a call to get to know them and their situation. For more than 15 years I have started with the same question: "Can you tell me a little bit about your current innovation program?"

Although I have posed that question more than one thousand times to thousands of different people in hundreds of different industries and organizations whose programs varied in their degree of development, the answers seem to have much in common and are startlingly consistent. Let's see if I can paraphrase what I've heard:

Recently the leader of our organization decided that innovation is absolutely the most important part of our [insert *principles, values, directives, mission, values statement, strategy,* or *beliefs*]. The whole company knows that innovation is important because last quarter our leader gave a presentation and the third slide in the 161-slide presentation stated that innovation is the key to our success. She even represented how important it was by illustrating it with a [insert *pillar, pyramid, photo of a light bulb with a question mark in it,* or *quote from Steve Jobs*]. In response, we have built our innovation program.

So far we have hired a chief innovation officer from outside of our industry; he seems to have worked at several companies in the last decade and we've decided that's a good thing. His job isn't that well defined because innovative people really don't like to be shackled by things like job descriptions. We are really excited to have him.

We hired an outside consulting firm to define the word *innovation* for our organization, our leader explained, because our culture, company, industry, and customers are so different from those of any other company. The outside firm charged us a ton of money after claiming to spend a lot of time in "research mode" in order to come up with a definition particular to us. As a joke a guy down the hall Googled our innovation definition and we were all a bit surprised that it was only two words different from 16 other organizations' definitions of innovation. Ironically, all of those companies had hired the same third-party consultant that we did.

Once we had our definition we had to get top-down buy-in, so we asked senior executives to volunteer some of their time to head up what we like to refer to as the Innovation Vetting Panel, or IVP. The members gather quarterly to discuss innovative strategies and they decide what ideas and innovations should receive moderate funding to go to the next step. Once I heard a guy in the cafeteria ask if the IVPs wear robes at their meetings and if they have some sort of secret headquarters or sanctum. I chuckled and said I wasn't really sure. But they probably do.

In an organization of our size we clearly couldn't put much pressure on a small number of execs, as their bandwidth is already quite low. So we created an enterprise-wide team of innovation advocates. We named that group of innovation leaders the I Team, so everyone would understand who they are and what they do. The *I* in I Team stand for *innovation*—and that move alone is awfully innovative.

We had our third-party consultant hire a third-party firm to develop an ideation receptacle portal—we call it an IRP—which is a place where people can deposit fresh ideas. What's really cool is that people can also go there and vote on which ideas they like. The third-party firm that our third-party consultant hired came up with a supercool way to rank the ideas: We use a series of red, yellow, and green buttons to allow the user to weigh in on the idea. We really feel that our IRP is state-of-the-art. So far we only have 7 percent participation, and many people have said that it seems as if it's simply a website in a survey we sent out, but our third-party consultant's third-party firm assured us that it was much more than that.

After taking all of this in, I ask, "So what are some of the results your innovation program has achieved?" Once again, I tend to get a consistent response:

It's funny you ask. Our chief financial officer had a quite similar question. You see, we are in a period of expense efficiency, or as we like to say, operation transformation, and the CFO is interested in identifying tangible and results-based return on investment from our innovation program. That question seemed to really irritate our chief innovation officer.

We've had some attrition in our I Team, as the members sometimes get frustrated that the ideas being generated aren't going to market fast enough. A couple of them have left the company to join small start-ups.

The most successful part of our innovation program seems to be our i'nnovation rally events. They are super well attended, and the energy level is great! We're not sure; however, if we will be able to continue having them, as the survey results showed that the attendees' motivation was tied greatly to the food served at the event.

This is the point in the conversation at which I typically drop the big question. "So, tell me about what your company is doing to help people behave more innovatively?" On the phone, there is always an awkward silence; in person, there is a bit of eye glazing and a far-off stare. In both cases the reply is usually the same: "What do you mean by *behavior*?"

I then get very complicated and scientific in my response, which is typically, "What I mean by behavior is, how do the people in your organization *act*? How do they treat each other? What does it feel like after people come up with ideas? What happens when an innovation attempt fails? How do people treat each other on conference calls or in brainstorming sessions? Does the vibe in the room ever change when certain individuals walk in? What I mean is: *How do people behave?*"

When it comes to a big, beautiful, exciting, but somewhat vague term like innovation, it is easy to migrate to the conceptual, high-level thinking at which many leaders operate on a daily basis, especially when the enterprise is concerned. And that is absolutely great and necessary for setting strategy, goals, and systemic approaches to becoming a more innovative organization.

However, we often forget about everyday behavior, because in a way it is so basic that the big thinkers—the super smart innovation architects—can assume that everyday behavior is a given that will automatically change once a great system is in place. The old saying "Everything looks like a nail to a hammer" can be an appropriate way to think about the manner in which innovation programs are structured—and often the teams who work on those programs forget a very basic ingredient of a successful innovation effort: *the people*—and all their fears, emotions, and humanness—who need to fuel it.

Although sometimes Steve Jobs is quoted too frequently, we are fans, and can't help but share the way he put it: "Innovation has nothing to do with how many R&D dollars you have. When Apple came up with the Mac, IBM was spending at least 100 times more on R&D. It's not about money. It's about the people you have, how you're led, and how much you get it."

Innovation is about people and their assumptions and subconscious thought patterns (a.k.a. their mindset) and their daily actions and habits that stem from that mindset (a.k.a. their behavior). Put all those together, add some procedures, rewards and penalties, social dynamics, unspoken rules—and a pinch of stress—and you get a wonderfully messy, organic, and complex environment. An environment in which behavior, not lip service (although words are also important), drives the results. If you fail to address that daily behavior, even the greatest strategy and plan to drive innovation are doomed to fail.

If the systems we create aren't rooted in a thorough understanding of the human interaction they are supposed to support they can actually deter the experience we want to create for our customers. Ryan Armbruster, experience lead and cofounder of Harken Health, is a passionate proponent of human-centered design—innovating with the end user, the patient, at the center of everything he does. Ryan is a pioneer and leader of human-centered service design and innovation in the healthcare industry, whose work includes significant roles at UnitedHealth Group and the Mayo Clinic. In addition, he teaches graduate and executive courses in service design and innovation at the University of Minnesota.

I wanted to bring in Ryan's perspective for a number of reasons. The first is that his innovation motivation starts in his heart. He's simply the type of person who wakes up every morning with an unquenchable yearning to find answers to questions that will help as many people as possible. He innovates for the sake of others, not for the sake of innovation.

He also is innovating in perhaps the most interesting space in American business today: a simple challenge we sometimes refer to as "just fixing healthcare." Even those of us who are outside the healthcare industry know that we're at a very critical place in a very critical time in an industry that embodies one of our most pressing national issues. The answers in healthcare will be a drastic departure from the current status quo. They will be disruptive, and they will come—in some version—at lightning speed compared to innovations in other industries, such as commercial airlines or network television.

Lastly, Ryan has lived in several worlds, from small innovation labs to giant hundred-thousand-person-plus companies. He is simultaneously a teacher and a student of innovation.

Here's a part of a recent conversation we had, which we'll revisit throughout the book:

John: Healthcare is a really great example of an industry that has increased the technology and systemization of its relationship with its customers, but it hasn't necessarily introduced a lot of behavioral innovation.

Ryan: It's an exciting time to be in healthcare, as we have been rapidly evolving on many different fronts, especially in terms of how healthcare and technology intersects, resulting in some groundbreaking innovations.

However, healthcare is complex—I think each of us at one time or another has experienced some level of frustration with the health system, which has been slower to adapt to a more customer-oriented society than our peers in other industry sectors.

John: So how can the healthcare industry change that dynamic?

Ryan: I think our goal over the next 5 or 10 years is to figure out how we design for caring.

I believe the vast majority of people in the healthcare sector are here to help people. They genuinely care about each person's experience and the need to do more to make healthcare easier to navigate and understand.

It also requires broadening our thinking and includes looking at other sectors—for example, taking a page out of what our peers in retail and consumer electronics have been doing over the last few years—when it comes to designing products and services tailored around a person's individual needs.

We're already seeing some of that thinking in healthcare and will likely see much more of it in the years to come.

John: That's been a focus of yours since the beginning.

Ryan: Absolutely. I got interested in healthcare because I was interested in caring for people. I was in school for that. I was thinking, do I want to be a doctor? Do I want to be a nurse? Then, as I started to get toward the end of my first bout of college, I tried to determine how I could make the biggest impact. That's what drove me into more of an administrative or business role in healthcare; that's the level at which you're making decisions that influence populations. In the traditional physician role, you're often working one-on-one. I thought I could make a bigger impact by taking my interest in helping people, particularly through healthcare, and going down the administrative path. Then I got into it and I realized, oh no, I don't like this at all, because all I do is sit in an office and think about numbers on spreadsheets, and that's not what healthcare leadership should be solely about.

John: So how did you decide to devote your career to changing behaviors in healthcare?

Ryan: I knew I could work with doctors and nurses and care professionals and help figure out how we could design an even better experience for people, so they're not only getting the care that our providers deliver, but we're also designing the systems, the resources, and the tools around these people with empathy in order to make it even more effective.

And that's exactly what Ryan did. We'll hear more from him about his story and his passion for innovation later.

Ryan Armbruster's journey is a great example of how difficult it can be to balance a focus on shifting behaviors with a focus on creating systems. The truth is that behavior change is hard: Most people resist change, and the organizational culture can be, and often is, at odds with the environment needed for innovation. In fact, some researchers—including Govindarajan and Trimble (Govindarajan and Trimble 2010)—argue that companies struggle with innovation not because of a lack of ideas but because they aren't able to implement them due to market, organizational, or cultural pressures.

The managerial culture that strives for efficiency, leanness, speed, and quality is often in conflict with the innovation culture that calls for space for experimentation, learning from mistakes, and time to make unexpected connections through exploration.

I've been a student of behavior my whole life, but over the past two decades I've been immersed deeply in how profoundly important behavior is in the innovation process by experiencing firsthand the ups and downs of entrepreneurship and through reinventing the oldest satirical comedy theater in the United States.

Here's our organization's story.

2

The Brave New Workshop:
A Journey of Fear and Discovery

Hazel
Hey, any plans for the weekend?

Thor
So far laundry is the most exciting thing on the list.

Hazel
Thrilling.

Thor
How about you?

Hazel
Thinking of either a movie or a comedy theater.

Thor
Wow, both sound fun. Action movie?

Hazel
No, heart-wrenching romantic drama about war, chronic illness, loss of the only person she loved.

Thor
Wow, sounds fun. Maybe the comedy show?

Hazel
I'm not sure, it's improv, what if they call on me to be involved on stage?

Thor
OMG, I had not thought of that. Plus they just make stuff up, I mean why would anyone pay for that? Don't you have other options?

Hazel
Well, there's always laundry.

Thor
Thank you for sharing in the epic fail that is my social life.

B ack in 1997 my soon-to-be wife, Jenni Lilledahl, and I took a huge risk and purchased the Brave New Workshop Comedy Theater (the BNW) from the legendary Dudley Riggs.

Dudley, a former circus performer, started the BNW in Minneapolis in 1958 with the motto Promiscuous Hostility, Positive Neutrality. Back then the idea of presenting social and political satire—based on real life, current events, and issues—in a comedy revue format seemed crazy. To make it comedy-only theater—one that presented an original ensemble-created production several times a year, without a dime of grant money—seemed less than a sure thing, and perhaps even shocking.

It's not a stretch to say that since then it has become a legendary comedy institution, in addition to being the oldest running satirical comedy theater in the United States. Alums of the BNW workshop stage include Louie Anderson (*Life with Louie*), Pat Proft (*Police Academy, The Naked Gun*), (now Senator) Al Franken (*Saturday Night Live*), Tom Davis (*Saturday Night Live*), Mo Collins (*Mad TV*), Peter MacNicol (*Ally McBeal, 24*), Melissa Peterman (*Reba*), Cedric Yarbrough (*Reno 911, The Boondocks*), and Rich Sommer (*Mad Men*).

Jenni and I met in one of Dudley's improvisation classes in 1992. We both had a passion for theater and a yearning to leave the corporate rat race. At the time, the theater boasted four full-time employees and annual revenues of $260,000. The school of improvisation was an ad hoc operation of cast members and alumni teaching sporadic classes, and corporate business was virtually nonexistent.

Right out of the gate we were looking for new and viable revenue streams, and the first was doing comedy shows for the Disney Cruise Line. After a multi-year, seven-figure contract to send casts onboard to perform 42 weekly improv shows, Disney ultimately decided to replace the shows with dueling piano performances. This exciting foray into the world of cruise ships proved to be a breakeven venture at best.

Exploring Expansion

In 1998, fueled by dreams of growth, we set our sights on moving the theater to the prime Calhoun Square location in the heart of Minneapolis's lively Uptown neighborhood to offer more amenities to theatergoers: namely, parking, restaurants, and restrooms. We invested nearly $500,000 into renovations, and we grew to 12 full-time employees and 15 part-timers.

The Calhoun Square theater opened in step with Brave New Workshop's fortieth anniversary, yet despite the BNW team's effort and creativity, the investment didn't pay off and attendance grew by only 6 percent. It was clear by the end of 2001 that the theater couldn't continue to support the staff and overhead costs. So in an effort to reduce expenses we moved back to the historic 2605 Hennepin Avenue location, determined to create a new revenue stream to support the organization and create a sustainable model.

I forgot to mention that Brave New Workshop is a self-funding arts organization. We have never pursued or taken grants or donations to support our theater operations. Our belief is that nonprofit and arts funding should go to more critical issues—the comedy and satire we provide, while healthy for the brain and providing lots of food for thought, can't compete with the need for sustenance, shelter, and health care. We also believe that the experiences we create should be such that people will want to pay for them. Additionally, we have always seen our organization as innovative enough to create a sustainable model for arts organizations that is less dependent on inconsistent public dollars.

Now, back to our story. While the Calhoun Square experiment was under way, Jenni poured her energy and vision into growing the school of improvisation from five students in 1997 to more than 200 students in 1999. Together we brought our passion for long-form improvisation to the Twin Cities area and established a weekly student performance showcase, which hosted more than 500 performances over the next 15 years.

Our passion to grow our theater audience prompted us to lease more space at the Palace Theater, across the river in St. Paul this time, where we managed two hit dinner theater shows: *Flanagan's Wake* and *Minnesota! It's Not Just for Lutherans Anymore*. But despite the popularity of both shows, the St. Paul nightlife didn't increase in energy or volume, and we closed our St. Paul location at the end of the lease.

Enter Corporate Services

Amid the theater ups and downs our motivation to build a sustainable business was unwavering. As early as 2000 we understood that the company's growth couldn't be funded solely by theater ticket revenue and bar sales. So our team started to experiment with the idea of a new business, featuring corporate speaking, training, and entertainment services. The idea was fueled by the testimonials of the students in our school of improvisation: They revealed that practicing the art form of improvisation brought tremendous benefits into their work and home lives. We laid the foundation of what is now known as Brave New Workshop's Creative Outreach, and I began testing out my prototype keynote speech on my former corporate real estate clients. For the next two years I spent the majority of my time and energy growing this new venture we called Brave New Communications (BNC), which was to bridge our know-how and talents with the business world.

The contraction in the local theater industry began to set in, and in 2002 the theater's annual attendance fell from 20,000 to 14,000 and the budget underwent a significant reduction. Our productions remained entertaining and innovative and were a seasonal favorite for Twin Cities locals. By 2009 the theater had gradually grown its attendance to 27,000. Regardless, until 2011 the theater continued to operate on a minimal budget and maintained annual losses of more than 10 percent per year, which were subsidized by the burgeoning corporate business.

Thankfully, the corporate-services side of the business boomed during the mid-to-late part of the first decade of the twenty-first century. I gained significant traction with global clients, including Microsoft, Hewlett Packard, Yahoo!, the Minnesota Timberwolves, Hilton Hotels, and PricewaterhouseCoopers. We expanded our offerings to include keynote speeches, corporate entertainment, corporate videos, training sessions, and emcee services. By 2007 the corporate services side had grown to six full-time members.

We met our original goal of $1 million in revenue in corporate services, and the model of a self-funding arts organization proved to be successful. My speaking fee grew from $500 to $15,000, and even amidst the recession our team continued to produce more than $1 million annually. In 2010 we rebranded as Brave New Workshop Creative Outreach. By 2012 my speaking fee had grown to $20,000.

We never stopped looking for new revenue streams or ways to be more efficient and effective in our work. In January of 2011 Jenni and I decided to purchase a building from the City of Minneapolis in a premier downtown location to house the comedy theater and develop a new rental event space aimed at increasing profitability. We also wanted a way to give back, so we announced Project 824, one of BNW's giving programs, which committed to 824 free uses of the space for community organizations.

In September of 2014 we made another big jump into the real estate space and purchased one more building in downtown Minneapolis to house our school of improvisation (the Student Union), our corporate training certification programs, and our offices. With two buildings across the street from each other we were able to create a campus where comedy, the art form of improvisation, and a mindset of discovery can be experienced viscerally through performances, classes, learning events, and customer service.

The Future Is Bright

After 18 years of growth, contraction, and then more growth, our team is well positioned to grow all aspects of our organization. We now have 20 full-time employees and 54 part-time employees. Revenues set new records, with the help of our new spaces and a new president for the entertainment side of the company. In 2015 we expect revenues from our combined entities to be $3.5 million.

So now you know the milestones along the Brave New Workshop's journey. It's been a heck of a ride. But what about the behind-the-scenes story? How did our winding path to success impact the people who made it happen? And how did my team's mindset and behaviors impact our journey? And exactly what does it all mean for you and your organization?

What's In It for Me?

As a way to give an example of innovative entrepreneurship, my clients have asked me to share my story and the 18-year growth journey of our company many times. As you've just read, the journey certainly hasn't been linear, consistent, or even predictable. There were times when our plans worked out and our strategies were well aligned. There were also times filled with dramatic highs and plunging lows, days when there was more desperation than hope, when survival was the only goal and profitability seemed like a far-off pipe dream.

After I share the store of our journey with an audience there are quite frequently floods of questions. The audience members seem to be looking for a magic formula, a shortcut, or a hidden secret. They're hoping that I can give them reliable answers that are applicable to any situation.

I can tell that they would love it if I would simply put up a Power-Point slide that says, "Here's a way to avoid making the mistakes I had to make and here are five simple steps to create an innovative culture and double-digit growth and profitability." I can also tell you that if I knew any of those things I'd be the first one to use them.

They want to know how we came up with some of our great ideas. They want to know how we were able to retain such great employees through unthinkable financial struggles. They want to know how we grew while the rest of our industry shrank. And they want to know what tools and systems and processes we used. All I can do is tell them the truth: We didn't use strategies, great business tools, or even exceptional talent. What helped us capitalize on the big opportunities was, in fact, *our mindset.*

Unfortunately, there isn't a guidebook to follow when it comes to buying the nation's longest-running comedy theater right before the digital age boom. There isn't a manual for creating a corporate training program based on the principles of an art form. There isn't a rule book for how to create brand recognition with C-level executives who have never heard of you or your theater. There isn't a website that gives you three easy steps for financing the growth of a company that is losing money. And there isn't a cheat sheet for keeping your employees focused and happy when it feels like the world is crumbling around you.

I go on to tell them that the only consistency in our growth story has been that we have stayed true to practicing and living a *mindset of discovery* as often as possible. Reflecting back on our ability to maintain that innovative mindset and commitment to the five behaviors that keep us grounded in it has given us many insights, which we will share with you in the chapters to come.

Clearly, this book's main impetus and focus is to use this mindset of discovery and the behaviors associated with it in the work place. But as I get older, and as my life deepens and broadens, I am realizing that the benefits of this mindset reach far beyond the business world and in many cases have more meaningful benefits in my non-work life.

Most people think about innovation as it relates to business. My understanding of innovation actually started when I was introduced to the art form of improvisation (much more on that later). As my business speaking and training career developed, almost all of my research, practice, and focus regarding innovation centered on increased productivity and success in large organizations. And although my consulting, content development, and speaking work still takes up the majority of my days, the mindset of discovery has shown itself to be of great value in other areas of my life:

As a husband. Like many relationships, our marriage has grown and changed and had highs and lows. But its core is still two people sharing lots of time, lots of tasks, and lots of goals and aspirations together. We are a lifelong improv scene, a lifelong collaboration, and a lifelong product development cycle.

I think I am a better husband than I was 20 years ago—I think I'm at my best as a husband when I am rooted in the mindset of discovery. The symptoms of that mindset in my marriage are the continuous curiosity about getting to know each other and the confidence with which we approach the unexpected challenges and heartaches that come with marriage and life. There is the appreciation for each other's points of view even when they are considerably different. And an expectation that the future will be different from what we can predict and that it will be just fine. I feel certain that Jenni would agree with all of this.

As a father. I thought I knew how to improvise quite well, and then when I became a dad I realized that parental improvisation was about 3 billion times harder and much more important than stage improvisation. I had improvised with numerous types of scene partners—but none so reliant and needy as a newborn or as curious as a toddler. None were as headstrong and sometimes defiant as a 6-year-old or as self-conscious and tender as a 12-year-old.

So to improvise and guide my two sons I have faithfully been able to fall back on this mindset of discovery. It has helped me to trust myself when there wasn't enough data about exactly what to do next. It greatly increased my ability to listen to them, sometimes about the most trivial—yet important—things. It made me sharpen my communication skills and realize that regardless of how I deliver messages, if they don't land—let alone impact the person I am communicating with—then I have not done my job. As a couple, Jenni and I did all of the typical things to educate ourselves on how to be good parents. But in hindsight I am most grateful for the mindset of discovery work I have done in other parts of my life, as I believe it has helped me the most as a parent. Now, if we can just keep these kids out of juvenile detention.

As a small business leader. The role of a small business leader is the one that probably resonates the most with readers—and the one I struggle with the most. This is when it's the hardest for me to walk the talk. This is also the role for which I am most grateful to have the mindset of discovery, at least to aspire to and guide me as I stumble through leading a small organization. If I had to identify the area of my life in which I spend the most time in a mindset of fear—the direct opposite of the mindset of discovery—it would be leading and managing a company.

It humbles me to have spent so much time learning and helping others to understand and live the mindset of discovery and yet not be able to do it in my own company nearly as often or as consistently as I would like. There are days when I feel like a fitness instructor who can't stay in shape. If I were a consultant to my own business I would easily be able to identify which behaviors I need to work on to become a better leader and manager of the wonderful people I employ. Living the mindset of discovery on a daily basis is a different challenge altogether. What I can say, however, is that this mindset of discovery has allowed me to honestly evaluate and observe my own behavior in a way that provides clear direction for what I need to do to get better at my job. I can also attest that as we migrated from a more general understanding of this mindset to a more sophisticated and well-defined learning model, I've been able to more regularly practice the specific behaviors I need to work on. Because of that I have some simple daily reminders and practices that I believe have made me a better leader of our organization than I was last year, or the year before, or the year before that. I hope my employees would agree.

The manifestation of this mindset has most clearly shown itself in my recent (in the past three years) ability to surrender control of several important aspects of our company and more clearly delegate and empower others. My commitment to allow others who are more capable than I am to run areas of the company that I used to run has greatly increased our company's productivity and profitability. That result feels like an obvious sign that I am spending more time in the mindset of discovery. The more I live in that mindset, the better our small company performs. I think my coworkers would describe it as—the more Sweeney lives in the mindset of discovery, the more it feels like he trusts us.

So with the few examples above, I've tried to answer the question that many of us have when reading a book like this one: "I understand that this will help me help my company, but what's in it for me?" For me it has been wonderfully surprising that this mindset, which we uncovered as a way to help other companies improve their performance, has given me insights and benefits and near miracles in my day-to-day life. It may sound trite, but the more I embrace the mindset of discovery, the happier I am, the richer my life seems, and the more productive I am as a citizen of this planet. I'm confident that it can have a similar impact on your life.

The reason I'm so confident is because of the way I've seen it impact my employees and clients, especially those who have developed a practice plan around the mindset that works best for them.

I have been a friend, partner, and fan of Gina Valenti for a long time. I have watched her—in her roles as vice president of owner services for Hilton Worldwide and vice president of brand culture and internal communications for the Hampton brand—create and implement ideas and innovative programs that actually create culture. That is one of the hardest tasks I know of, especially when the team you are trying to help numbers 60,000 people who are not direct employees.

We have been fortunate enough to partner with her on dozens of initiatives throughout the years. I have always been amazed by her drive, her focus, and her genuine compassion and desire to help the team members of Hampton. She has taught me a ton of things about how to help and lead people toward their best selves.

Gina understands that it is the little things done well and consistently that lead to behavior change and results. She is hands-on and always makes sure that she has lived the situation before she makes recommendations and develops the innovation for the solution.

She is also an amazing example of being a lifelong student. Every time I connect with her she has something new to tell me that she has just read or experienced. She especially loves new information that can be backed up by research and results. She is always in the mode of "What can I absorb next?"

Perhaps my favorite thing about her is how passionate she is about lifting people up and helping them recognize and live their strengths. She does this by providing them with the tools they'll use for their journey, and she recognizes them when they do well. But the most impressive thing she does both helps those she connects with and spreads innovation. Gina finds people who are doing great things and then shines a huge light on them so that they feel great about themselves and their strengths and so that their best practice and innovation can be shared.

Gina is a phenomenal example of someone who lives the concepts we discuss in this book, and she has changed her teammates' and her own life in the process. I am grateful to have this chance to shine a light on her and share her insights with you.

John: Let's say someone is 30 years old and she's asking herself, "Hmm, what can I do to move away from fear? What can I do to grow my own confidence?" All of a sudden, Gina Valenti shows up and says, "Well, listen my friend! Here's some advice about how to live a life of asking what you can do instead of what you can't!" What kind of advice would you have for a young businessperson?

Gina: I'll give you my advice for my young self, because I think that if I could go back and be 30 again, what I would tell my 30-year-old self is, "Stop taking everything so seriously."

Take that "The world feels like it's weighing on your shoulders and nothing will exist unless you solve it" feeling and lighten up and know that the answers are all out there. And that the exciting part is to discover them. Be curious and know that it's all out there just for your choosing. You have more power in your hands than you can imagine, and you get to design the future. You just have to pick up the pen and start doing it, and just let go of the fear of what can't be, and celebrate what can be, and be grateful. The more, personally, I am grateful for what I have, the more abundance and the more possibility I see. I wish I knew that as a 30-year-old!

Some like to call innovation progress, and I agree. Without continuing to rethink old paradigms and find new solutions to current problems, stagnation—and eventual demise—will ensue. In our current interconnected, lightning-fast world that's full of tremendous, complex challenges, we have to take an active role in contributing our insights and putting our ideas in motion in order to collectively create the world we want to live in.

As technologist and writer Ramez Naam puts it, "Knowledge and ideas are the most important, unlimited resource on the planet." Honing a mindset of discovery and practicing innovation behaviors on a daily basis is the best way we can ensure that future generations will inherit a healthy planet and sustainable society that supports prosperity and happiness for all its members.

3

The Mindset of Discovery:
Improvisational Roots

Moira
How's the presentation coming?

Ashok
Okay. I am really trying to take a different approach.

Moira
How so?

Ashok
I want to be conversational instead of presentational.

Moira
Cool. Almost like improv.

Ashok
Exactly. I mean, kind of like improv.

Moira
Yep, like off the top of your head, spontaneous, without a net!

Ashok
Sort of. I do have 23 note cards though.

Moira
Right – better safe than sorry, but not corporate-y sounding drool fest, right?

Ashok
No way. I mean beyond the stuff on the brand and compliance and the new operational excellence program description and the onboarding guide that HR included.

Moira
Of course, but not like a typical deck-driven, try-to-pay-attention-but-fall-asleep-on-your-forearm type, soul-thief PowerPoint thing.

Ashok
Not a chance, I am using a little PowerPoint just to reinforce some of my disruptive provocations.

Moira
Awesome, any audience interaction?

Ashok
A ton! I have a really cool Q&A graphic on slide 78 with *seven* question marks!

Moira
Supercool. I hope the audience can step up and engage.

T he definition of the mindset of discovery emerged from more than 55 years of improvising off and on stage at the Brave New Workshop. Without this kind of mindset, it's nearly impossible to create and collaborate at the rapid pace our stage requires with the added stress of a live audience. As I shared earlier, we would have failed at growing and prospering as a business if we hadn't embraced this mindset. Improvisation has been a force in my life for 23 years, and I have found it to be an amazing vehicle to practice the behaviors and mindset needed for successful innovation.

The mashup of improvisation in the corporate world has been a part of my life since 1992. I had begun to take improvisational classes as a way to take a break each week from what was beginning to feel like what some people call the grind—essentially, the burnout of the day-to-day activities of a pretty typical corporate job. I was working for a wonderful corporate real estate firm that specialized in full-service relocation and construction management. We found the best places for companies to have offices and conduct their business and then beat up landlords and construction companies on behalf of our clients, who would then become tenants or buyers. I was surrounded by lots of great people, but the competitive stress and high-profile lifestyle were both exciting and draining. I was young (25) and was about to have everything I thought I was supposed to be chasing: a great house, a high-paying job, big opportunities for career advancement, and access to all the things a fast-moving, hard-charging young executive wanted.

And then, once a week for three hours, I would find myself in an improvisational acting class in a tiny storefront theater. There were weeks when it felt as if I were stepping through a portal to an alternate dimension—as if I were walking into a different world. It wasn't just the people—although they were very different from the people I was spending my days with on the fortieth floor of a skyscraper in downtown Minneapolis. It was the art form, its rules of engagement, its cultural norms, and its operational and logistical manufacturing process. It was what I know now as the culture of "Yes, And!"

There were so many aspects of this world and of this art form that contrasted with what I was learning, practicing, and participating in during my work hours. In hindsight, that contrast made even more of an impact because I worked at a really progressive organization with really smart people. I liked working where I was, and what I did. The level of confidence of the people I was surrounded by in my day job was spectacular. There was an unbelievable striving for excellence and a work ethic that still impresses me. Yet this new and different approach to getting things done that I learned via improv was completely addicting.

I think one of the main reasons that the improvisational approach was so attractive to me is because it complemented many of the things that came naturally to me—and at an emotional level, many of the things that people told me I should *stop* doing, or do differently. I often joke that when I am improvising on stage, I am doing almost everything I was told not to do during my entire academic career. "For crying out loud, Sweeney, put down the class gerbil, and get off my desk." This strange and liberating new set of life rules and productive processes allowed me to be my true self, the person I most enjoyed being—the same person that I had been told *not to be* for decades.

I tell you this because I wanted to be honest about the fact that my love affair with improvisation is very personal. Not everyone might have such a huge attraction to it. But still, as I think back to those first improvisational classes, there were so many simple, yet profound, things that I was learning and experiencing that I carry with me today, and that have helped me in my business life and in becoming who I am.

A few of the things that seemed so startling, and perhaps so contrary to what I needed to do to succeed at work, stick out in my mind.

Granted this was 1992, and many of the status quo and traditional business approaches and beliefs were much different than they are today, but here's what I learned:

- *Make everyone on stage look better than you at all times.* Making others look better seemed a bit different than the mentality of being the most valuable player and always trying to impress your boss and wow your clients so you can get ahead that I was taught and was practicing at the time.
- *Reframe mistakes as steppingstones toward success.* Reframing mistakes as instrumental in achieving success was the beginning of my understanding of how dreadfully frightened I was of making mistakes. It helped me realize that the shame and punishment I suffered from being wrong that I had experienced in my life was really affecting my ability to be innovative.
- *The fastest way to build something is to be in a culture of agreement.* Collaboration represented a much different approach from the combative, winner-takes-all, aggressive approach I had embraced for many years.
- *Serving your teammates and the audience will lead to far greater success than serving yourself.* The service mentality had certainly been introduced to me at church; however, at that point I believed that there was a completely different set of rules for how to win in business.

There were countless things that I learned from my early days in the business world, and I'm grateful for those lessons and the people I worked with. I often say, however, that it would've been valuable—and a lot more fun—to have learned about improvisation and to have begun operating according to the mindset of discovery before I started my career in real estate.

I'm also tremendously grateful for the wonderful contrasts that these two worlds provided to me. I learned fast by having one foot in each world. It was an exciting time in my life and in many ways a precursor to what I am doing now. I went from only the corporate world to both the corporate world and the improvisational world to just the improvisational world—and for the past 15 years back to the wonderful combination of both. Looking back I can appreciate that the journey probably should have gone just as it did. However, in the beginning I had no idea where the road was leading.

Although the intention of this book is not to teach someone how to improvise, especially on stage, it's important to at least explain why improvisational performance has been such an essential part of developing the mindset of discovery and our understanding of how that mindset can help others offstage. Performance improvisation is a wonderful metaphor, an amazing piece of science, humanity, and process that we can dissect and learn from. We are also big fans of the liberal arts learning model that asks us to expose ourselves to diverse areas of study and to experiment with various schools of thought and worldviews.

I spent a great deal of time and effort learning improvisation for its most obvious purpose: to perform improvisational comedy. But I have to admit that this art form has taught me much more about workplace productivity and personal development than it has about stage performance. Taking several years of one's life to dive in and focus entirely on an art form and culture is rare in the typical career path; however, that's exactly what I was given the opportunity to do. After six years in corporate real estate, I spent four solid years reading, listening, practicing, and performing the art form of improvisation without any other distractions in my life. I was taking classes at some of the best improvisational schools on the planet, with some of the best improvisers, from some of the best teachers.

Many times the combination of class, practice, and performance would take 60 to 80 hours of my week. The focus and complete emergence I had the privilege of experiencing during those years was remarkable—truly a blessing. Regardless of whether you're lucky enough to be able to dive in that deeply or not, I would like to share a few of my condensed thoughts on why I feel improvisation is a great metaphor and set of principles to contemplate, translate, and apply to one's life and one's career.

If you have seen an improvisational performance, then you will know that our basic job as improvisers is to:

1. *Ask our customers* (the audience members) what they need, what they would like us to create for them, and what is important to

them. These things come from an audience suggestion that we use as inspiration to build the improvisational scene.

2. *Create roles* and determine who we are going to be in the scene. What is our point of view and what will we take responsibility for constructing or accomplishing within the scene? We call that our declaration.

3. *Listen to and understand* our scene partners' and teammates' declarations so that we can understand the roles they will play and how we will all work together.

4. *Create and share ideas* of what the scene could be about while moving the scene forward without a brainstorming session, let alone the time to analyze the ideas' viability.

5. Arrive at *the scene's core truth* and choose that as our catalyst for what we will build.

6. Achieve *complete buy-in* of that truth from the entire team.

7. Create exponentially a *prototype* of the next part of the scene every few seconds.

8. *Listen to each other and the audience* for direction and inspiration while continuing to make lightning-fast decisions regarding what the scene will be about and where it will go.

9. *Develop a piece of entertainment* that can compete with the myriad of other available entertainment options, including the free-of-charge and always-innovating Internet.

10. All of this, with a typical start-to-finish production *cycle of three to five minutes.*

Whew. So although the comparison between an improvisational scene and a productive workplace or fulfilled life is certainly not an apples-to-apples comparison, there are endless lessons to learn from this art form. It provides us with a simplified version of human interaction in short time segments, a unique lab environment that identifies and accentuates the key behaviors needed for the high levels of collaboration and innovation the audience requires.

In deconstructing and analyzing improvisation, there is enough content for an entirely separate book, and others have done so; that's not our purpose here.

For now there is only one aspect of our examination of improvisation that we would ask you to embrace. Even in improvisation's imperfection, even in its flawed process and oftentimes imperfect results, if one is to be successful in performing it, the single most important thing an improviser must do is to *embrace and live the mindset of discovery while on stage*. Throughout the book we'll make references to the art form of improvisation and use them as a way to illustrate and provide examples of how the behaviors and mindset of discovery look in their purest form, without the added complexity created by reality and life circumstances.

4

The Art of Practice

Bobby
How did the coaching session go, now that you are a certified mentor?!

Brady
Fail.

Bobby
How come? Did she freak?

Brady
Oh no, she was great, I just completely fell apart. I mean I was a head case!

Bobby
How so?

Brady
Oh, I don't know; how about, sweating, stumbling, forgetting, and stalling?

Bobby
Did you get your points across to her?

Brady
Thank goodness I had filled out her quarterly evaluation sheet, because I don't think she could understand any of the "nervous as a 12-year-old at his first dance" ridiculousness that was coming out of my mouth.

Bobby
I thought you had gone through an enterprise-learning-approved coaching certification class?

Brady
I did, it was a two hour e-learning so I just clicked through.

Bobby
Have you been practicing what you are supposed to be doing in the coaching sessions?

Brady
Yeah, right — when would I have time for that?

Bobby
Good point; why do you think it went so poorly?

Brady
I am not sure, I followed the steps on the sheet but I just wigged out!

Bobby
Maybe it was the location—where were you?

Brady
Conference room 342E.

Bobby
What were you wearing?

Brady
Just the standard suit and tie?

Bobby
It sounds as if you did all the right things. When's the next time you are doing one?

Brady
1:30 this afternoon.

Bobby
I am sure you will do fine.

I mprovisation has obviously given me some life-changing insights and is deeply ingrained in my past and current workplaces. However, I also believe in its value to all organizations, big and small, and to humanity in general, because of a very simple and practical reason: *It's a great way to practice key behaviors in a safe environment.*

Our school of improvisation has two specific educational tracks: One for folks interested in performing improvisation (a very small percentage of our adult students) and one for individuals who are simply taking improvisational classes to better their lives. They come to us for a few hours a week, typically for 18 months or so. The gratitude and appreciation they share with us is more than enough proof to me that improvisation is a great way to practice the most basic of life skills and perhaps some of the most enjoyable of life's hacks.

Part of the reason I think it is so effective is because it is active. Yes, the information and theory behind any behavioral change is important; however, when it comes to things such as becoming a better communicator, being more comfortable with risks, building one's confidence, or reducing the judgment with which we approach others, we need to put ourselves in scenarios with other humans to truly experience—and most importantly, *practice*—the meaning behind the information and theory.

Improvisation allows us to undertake some of these difficult, and perhaps even risky, behavior improvements off-line, away from our customers, away from the people we generally interact with in our lives. If life is the game on Friday night, then improv can be the practice that leads up to the game.

By its very nature, improvisation and its practice demand the creation of a safe environment. This is a bonus to the practice. How often do we know exactly what we need to do to improve our behavior—yet don't do it because it somehow doesn't feel safe? Every improvisational class at the Brave New Workshop Student Union creates and stresses the importance of a safe environment for all of its students. The goal of an improvisational class is to first create a safe environment and then gently encourage all the students to jump in and *practice, practice, practice.*

The Science Behind the Approach

Over the last few years, a growing body of research has supported the notion of using improvisation as an effective way to practice key behaviors.

Any learning and behavioral change has to begin by increasing our self-awareness and recognizing already-existing habits or thought patterns. Improvisation is an excellent vehicle to drive self-awareness, as the results of a four-year study of using improvisation in leadership programming in Australia clearly demonstrate.

According to the Australian researcher, "The method acted to enhance participants' focus on cognitive behavioral awareness. It provided an environment in which participants expanded their expressive emotional palette and also revealed possibilities for the translation of negative emotions like anxiety and confusion into creative energy by harnessing their reactive energy and thus enabling them to slow down their response rate, and in some cases to develop the capacity to choose their responses when under pressure" (Dennis 2014). In other words, the practice of improvisation allowed these leaders to know themselves better and make better choices.

According to neuroscientist Dr. Charles Limb, "there's also evidence that improvisation has effects on the brain. Neuroimaging studies have shown that when improvising, we use profoundly different parts of our brain than when performing from memory" (Liu et al. 2012). In fact, "during improv, the brain deactivates the area involved in self-censoring, while cranking up the region linked with self-expression" (Limb 2008).

The ability to quiet down the inner critic and decrease self-judgment is a key element of transitioning into the mindset of discovery. This helps us to share our ideas and opinions more frequently and freely, especially when we're on the spot or in unexpected circumstances. It improves the information flow within the organization and counteracts some fear-triggered, unproductive behaviors.

Practicing the Mechanics of Acceptance and Recognition

In his 10 years of studying theatrical improvisation and the implications of improvisational teams on innovation, Dr. Keith Sawyer has found that a key aspect of improvisation is its "collaborative emergence" characterized by (1) unpredictable outcome, (2) a moment-to-moment contingency (meaning that one person's actions are dependent on those of their teammates), (3) the interactional effect (that any given action can be changed by the subsequent actions of other participants), and (4) collaborative process in which each participant contributes equally (Sawyer and Dezutter 2009).

That interdependence between interacting team members creates a wonderful sense of valuing others' ideas and a true belief in the power of the group. But how does that apply in the real world? A 2014 survey by the American Psychological Association shows that "whether or not employees feel valued is a huge differentiation. Ninety-two percent of employees who feel valued say they're satisfied with their jobs compared with 29 percent of those who don't feel valued" (Excellence 2014).

We all know that how we play with others, function in a team, communicate, and collaborate is key to the success of innovation. In his book *Group Genius*, Sawyer shares case studies of diverse organizations that embrace improvisation as part of their innovation process. While they employ bursts of planning, they tend to do a lot more executing and experimentation, which is the reason for their innovation success. Sawyer shares that "improvisational teams are the building blocks of innovative organizations, and organizations that can successfully build improvisational teams will be more likely to innovate effectively" (Sawyer 2007).

Weaving Practice into Everyday Life

The beauty of improvisation is that its lessons seep into our lives almost unnoticeably. However, it's certainly not the only model for creating ways to incorporate behavioral practice in our everyday routine. We sought another example of how to address the challenges associated with incorporating behavioral practice into our busy schedules; this one comes from an ancient spiritual tradition.

Sr. Laureen Virnig, OSB (Order of St. Benedict), is a Benedictine nun who spends her days helping laypeople on a spiritual journey—the oblate way of life—that leans heavily on a fifteen-century-old list of practices called the Rule of St. Benedict. She has had a wonderfully diverse life and career journey, with five main ministries that have been part of her professional life: elementary school teacher, religious education director, pastoral associate, postulant and novice director, and currently, director of oblates. "Lessons from all of these have come together like threads to make the weaving of my present work as oblate director an enjoyable experience," she says.

As oblate director, she's in charge of a wonderful and transformative experience called the oblate way of life. Oblates are women or men who associate themselves with a monastery (in this case, Saint Benedict's Monastery in St. Joseph, Minnesota) and who follow the Rule of Benedict, incorporating practices of Benedictine spirituality into their daily lives. Christians of all faith denominations may become oblates and may be married or single. It allows the layperson to learn and embrace the Benedictine spirituality. There are several practices that shape Benedictine spirituality. It is the daily *practice* of these—including awareness of God, hospitality, community, service to others, stability of heart, being in right relationship, stewardship of resources, commitment for growth, silence, mindfulness, moderation in all things, humility, and listening—that leads to these practices becoming a "way of life."

Sister Virnig shares her guidance on the oblate's journey through a series of teachings and reading and questions called *weavings*. "The weaving image is a significant one for me because it speaks of integration, of taking the familiar and creating something new and, hopefully, life-giving, and then sharing it," she says.

To me, that sounds like one definition of innovation.

I've known Sister Virnig for decades, and she's taught me much in our time together. She reminds me that doing a little each day is essential to a behavior becoming habitual. She is a wonderful example of the fact that a clear set of defined behaviors is the key to any human transformation. The oblate way of life provides a perfect blend of guidelines, flexibility, and opportunity for self-reflection. It provides a path that is made from the footsteps of the person taking the journey.

John: I'm so interested in the patience that it takes for daily simple practices to change your behavior, to transform you, to bring you closer to yourself—because that's the big battle that we have in business. We love a program as long as it can show results in 60 days. Are people going to be different in 60 days? My answer is, I don't think so. It can take a lot longer than that to really stick.

You've been following this way of life since you became a nun, right?

Sr. Virnig: Yes—I've been in the monastic way of life for 57 years now. Where I was when I came here is not where I am today. It's a process. I think of that quotation we hear every Good Friday, "God's faithfulness is new every morning." Some days I can't do so well; for example, I sometimes take care of my grandnephew while his brothers are in school. I can't say I always pray as much as I should while he's here; but then I think, I can begin again tomorrow. Maybe I wasn't practicing prayer as much as I was practicing hospitality and patience and presence.

There are many Benedictine practices. I can't hold all of them at the same time. Sometimes I can, but I would focus especially on one for a week. I say, "I'm really going to try this and something's going to happen." Think about a rock that is constantly under dripping water; it's bound to get shaped in some way, some little indentation or some change. I think the human heart is like that, too. That repeated practice changes its shape. And that's the whole thing about Benedictine spirituality—practice. Not being perfect. I need to remember each morning God's love is new. Benedict says to never despair of God's mercy. It's not about being perfect, but beginning again.

John: The struggle for people in the corporate world to make innovation part of who they are—or at least the excuse—is, "I'm sorry,

I'm a salesperson at a major corporation, so I'm too busy selling and meeting with my clients and meeting my numbers to work on being innovative as well." But you're saying this way of life isn't a tangential or separate set of things; that if someone can do it daily, then the weaving starts.

Sr. Virnig: This person is so busy being a salesman that he can't do whatever. But can't he weave in being in a "right relationship" with people by being hospitable and friendly and welcoming?

John: And in our world, can he be weaving innovation in by being innovative in his relationships with his clients? How he sells? How he declares his product knowledge? A push-back to his statement is: "We're going to have a set of people we're going to call innovators and they're going to be in the innovation department. And what they do is come up with new ideas and build innovation for our company. Then we have finance, then we have sales, then we have operations, then we have HR and logistics." It creates silos.

Sr. Virnig: Everyone works in her little box. So, it's all about practice. You still want to continue on. With respect to the oblate way of life, we ask whether you want to commit to this way of life. Nobody's checking up on you saying, "You did this, you didn't do this." But if you want to go on, you're faithfully living it. And not necessarily every day; things happen. But every morning, you can start again. It's about doing whatever you are doing to the best degree you are able to.

John: Sometimes, someone will get an annual review from his boss that might say something like, "You need to increase your innovation skills and be more innovative. We'll talk about that again next quarter." So he has 90 days. And he feels this pressure, and he worries that he might not get a raise or promotion if he doesn't meet this objective that says, "I'm now more innovative." I hear this a lot from my clients. "Can you give us something that will make us more innovative? A magic pill or silver bullet?"

That's why I keep going back to the practice. The transformation can't really occur unless you do the practice.

Sr. Virnig: It's like a seed that needs to be nurtured. It needs sunshine and rain and nutrients.

We all have people in our lives who somehow manage to improve our perspectives; after we are with them, things are clear and make more sense. And we seem to know what we ought to do a little bit more than we did before we were with them. Sr. Virnig is one of those people for me.

One of my favorite moments of our interview was when I told her that sometimes in my work, people tell me that they don't think they are innovative or creative. She laughed and shook her head; she knows this all too well, since she is in the business of helping us get out of our own way. She knows that people can fool themselves into being less than their own potential.

Her belief system is firmly rooted in the premise that all of us are created with endless possibility. I asked her to keep me in her thoughts as I struggled to write this book; she told me that if I practiced listening, the book would come to me. I didn't know whom she wanted me to listen to at first, but then I realized that she meant that I should listen to my inner voice—to be self-reflective. When I told her my mind was racing hard with the deadline of the book looming, she reminded me that the words *listen* and *silent* have the same letters for a reason.

Thank you, Sister.

5

The Mindset of Fear

Paul
What's up?

Doug
Not much, what are you doing this weekend?

Paul
Don't laugh – but I'm thinking of taking a dance and movement class.

Doug
Seriously?

Paul
Seriously. In my review, I got a low score for engagement with others. They said I was "physically stoic."

Doug
Who isn't?

Paul
Right? Anyhow, I was thinking maybe a class like this could help me practice being more comfortable with my own body?

Doug
Have you told anybody?

Paul
Just you, why?

Doug
Don't take this the wrong way, but we are bankers. Do you want people to know that you move and dance?

Paul
Gotcha. Maybe there's a good book on corporate presence or an app for this this type of thing?

Doug
Good idea. Plus, if you don't take the class, you'll have your Sunday afternoons back to catch up on work.

In theory, there is nothing easier than improvisation. After all, you don't have to prepare or think ahead; you only need to be present in the moment, pay attention to what is happening around you, and react from a place of authenticity. In fact, improvisation demands *only* engagement and authenticity.

However, over more than 55 years of teaching people how to improvise we have found that there is one major barrier to finding the joy of improvisation.

Fear of failure.

When fear sets in, an internal monologue takes over the brain of even the most rational, confident, and competent individual:

What if I can't do it?

What if I draw a blank?

What if I let others down?

What if people think I'm stupid?

What if I lose my team's respect?

What if I say something offensive?

And the most common one:

What if I let myself down and my performance doesn't match up to my expectations for myself and the success I have had so far in life?

Fear of failure can be a paralyzing, time-consuming, heart-wrenching, or stomach-sinking experience, which too many of us have spent energy feeding—or, depending on the day—fighting. Unfortunately, it often lives on beyond the stage and the improvisational classroom or training session.

Of course, fear is an integral part of the human experience; it has clear survival and evolutionary purposes. In fact, as Caltech professor Ralph Adolphs shared in a recent radio interview, we are wired to feel fear often and to be very sensitive to threats so that we won't miss any. As a result, often we feel fear instantly even when there is no real danger (Adolphs 2015).

The problem, according to Adolphs, is that our modern world triggers our fear constantly in ways that our natural world doesn't. Our physiology sounds the alarm often: More often than it needs to. In our work, we've seen that take shape as irrational fears and self-imposed mental barriers, which cause distraction and hurt productivity.

We see fear manifest itself in different ways and varying degrees in most of the students and learners we work with on a daily basis. Everyone has a different story and a different monster to battle, but the common thread is this: We can all live happier and more productive lives if we are able to focus on what we care about most and minimize the time and energy we spend on worrying about things we can't control.

In addition to draining our time and energy, fear of failure can have some real economic impacts, especially when:

- You refuse a stretch opportunity because you can't predict the future.
- You don't participate in innovation events or activities because you don't perceive yourself as capable.
- You don't pursue a salary negotiation because you hate to be perceived as too aggressive.
- You never share your idea because it's too out of the box.
- You don't talk about the great work you do because people should just know.
- You don't ask for the flextime arrangement you need because you can do it all.
- You suppress your dream of starting a business.
- You don't pursue a promotion.

We want to show you how you can make the fear of failure irrelevant and transform that negative emotion into a productive drive that can allow you to perform to the best of your ability and maximize the opportunities that life presents you with.

The magic of practicing improvisation is that it provides a framework and a path for transforming

Fear of failure

into

excitement to discover

It can mean discovering new thought processes, discovering a new perspective during a difficult conversation, discovering how much you have in common with someone you don't know, discovering how capable you are on the other side of change, discovering a journey toward a better world, or discovering a new opportunity or venture.

This mindset of discovery is not about being an extrovert or introvert, quiet or loud, smart or silly. It's not about being on stage or being a comedy star. And it's not only a fun way to explore your creative side.

The mindset of discovery is a choice to not spend a disproportionate amount of time or energy on fear and to live a life of engagement, authenticity, and forward-looking action.

Moving Away from Fear

This past spring Jenni and I decided to take our sons on a civil-rights tour for spring break. We started in Memphis, then went on to Birmingham, Montgomery, and Selma. We visited more than a dozen museums and churches. We learned a lot and had great conversations in the car as a family and with the people we met on the journey. We knew it would be an educational vacation; we didn't know it would be life changing.

One of the great things that happened on our trip was that midway through, I received word from the people at Wiley that they had accepted my idea and were going to move ahead with the book you are currently reading. We had a great family celebration when we heard the news.

Forty-eight hours later, we found ourselves at the Dexter Avenue King Memorial Baptist Church in Montgomery, Alabama, for the 3:00 P.M. tour. Unfortunately, it was 3:15 P.M. I knocked on the front door and I called the number on the sign, but no luck. Then opportunity presented itself as two members of the staff were rolling some tables and chairs from the administrative offices to the door of the lower level. Now if there is one thing you learn when you own a theater, it's how to move and set up chairs. Off we went to offer our help and to gain entrance to the church—a win-win! Once inside we could hear a woman's beautiful voice singing from the upper level of the church. We got the tables in place and headed up for the tail end of the tour.

We entered the rear of the upper church and were immediately greeted by the tour leader, Wanda Howard Battle. Her eyes were bright, her smile was contagious, and she glowed with the love she had for life and the excitement of unexpectedly seeing us. She asked us our names and where we were from. She instantly made us feel welcome. She finished up the last part of the historical information about the church and Dr. King and told us she would be happy to share with us later the beginning of the tour that we had missed.

Then something more than coincidental happened. (Remember that just 48 hours earlier I had received the great news that I was going to write and publish a book about helping people to move from fear to discovery.) Miss Wanda told the group that what Dr. King and the civil rights movement did was to help people *turn away from fear*. She said that people realized that they needed to learn and practice turning away from fear. She then told a very personal story about how she had learned this herself. She said that once she decided to stop living in fear her life changed. She found more opportunity, more connections, and more ways to help others. She said that her life had blossomed.

As you can imagine, I was almost in a state of shock. This amazing woman, whom I had never met, was sharing her story of *moving from fear to discovery* with such inspiration and authenticity that it touched my heart and soul. I was teary-eyed and emotional; this certainly felt as if it was a bit more than serendipity.

I thanked Wanda for our meeting and her message. I told her about the book, about our theater, and about my work. I told her about how passionate I was about helping people move from fear to discovery. She was so kind and humble. She then gave us a private tour of Dr. King's office. What a spectacular way to end our first meeting with Miss Wanda.

She truly lives the premise of this book. She is a servant to others and a testimony to the possibility and potential that can come to anyone who chooses to practice and who tries to live in the mindset of discovery. I'm honored to be able to share her story with you:

Wanda: I've learned some really valuable lessons through my journey. So many times you can put a face on, even on your inner self. But it's a pretentious face of not really knowing who you really are and why you've been called to this planet and what your work really is and what difference it's really making. Not until I really got that was I able to step out of that place of fear.

It came through me being challenged. Now I understand it better. Because we're always learning on this journey of life.

John: Tell us the story you shared with me in Montgomery.

Wanda: I used to be very intimidated. Because I have a sister who's very smart. And most of my sisters are really brilliant in their own way. But this particular sister has a PhD. She has a very bold, courageous personality. I would sit quiet because I didn't think I had anything of substance or importance to say.

I was also awfully intimidated by people who seemed to know God in a way that I thought I could never have a relationship with God in that way. I didn't know that He would answer my prayers like that. I wasn't sure of that. Then, I guess I used to care about whether people liked me or not.

I put on this face and wore a certain face to others that I wanted them to see, or what I perceived I wanted to show them. Eleven years ago, the Lord challenged me. He told me to speak to a situation that was going on that involved these people. He said, "Wanda, I need you to just state a position." And I told Him, "I'm not doing that." And He said, "I need you to just state a position." And I said, "No. I'm not doing it."

He let me see what happened because I didn't speak to the matter. It allowed some things to happen that really didn't have to. It devastated me. I made up my mind, and said, "God, if you help me, I will never be afraid of another person or thing again."

It was as if I stepped over a door threshold just to the other side. What that represented to me was that the wall of fear that was inside of me came down. And when it came down everything about my life changed. The way I see myself has changed. I understand the gifts of God within me. I've sung since I was five years of age. I think that was the youngest I can remember singing.

A TV producer had asked me for a year and a half to come and record music for them. I would tell them no. Because inside, I was telling myself, "Girl, your voice isn't good enough to go and get on television." But when the wall of fear came down, I stepped into that place and I've been recording for them for two years now.

John: And now thousands of people can hear your beautiful voice because of that.

Wanda: Because the one thing that fear does, it makes things seem so gigantic and unconquerable. But when the Spirit comes down and there's nothing but love and freedom, it's so simple. Now I look back and I wonder why was I so afraid to be who God had created me to be? Why was I so intimidated by other people?

Now, what it has done, it allows me to appreciate the gifts that lie within my sister and other people. And I appreciate them. God has used me to go back and be a blessing to them.

Her story is so simple, and so powerful. And clearly, her motivation in taking down the wall of fear was her personal faith in God. But each of us can find our own motivation in whatever works for us. What's most important about Miss Wanda's story is that it was her truth, her choice—an inspiring example of how leaving fear behind can transform our lives. We'll hear more from Wanda later in the book.

Fear in the Workplace

Just like in any other area of our lives, fear shows up at work. In fact, this mindset acts as an impetus for our work with many of our clients. It seems to be the squeaky wheel; when things aren't going well, the symptoms become more obvious. Our clients almost always contact us when things are going less than perfectly in their world. Not many times in the past 15 years has a client called and said, "Things are going exactly as they should around here; come on over and do some training."

Statistics back our observation. Recent research from the American Psychological Association shows that the majority of Americans experience a significant amount of stress (this likely doesn't come as a surprise to anyone). In a 2014 survey, 67 percent of those surveyed reported experiencing emotional symptoms of stress and 72 percent reported experiencing physical symptoms of stress (Anderson et al. 2014). In the same survey, 69 percent of those surveyed reported work as a source of stress (Anderson et al. 2014). In a 2012 survey by Accountemps, only 3 percent of 420 office-based employees called themselves fearless, and the number one fear of employees (28 percent) was of making a mistake (Accountemps 2012).

While it's clear that stress and fear are prevalent, what's not clear is what we're doing about it. Only 35 percent of those surveyed said they are doing an excellent or very good job of managing stress and 44 percent said they aren't doing enough or aren't sure whether they are doing enough to manage their stress. Yet 19 percent of Americans said they never engage in stress-management activities (Anderson et al. 2014).

The organizational implications of fear and stress are significant. Research shows that anxious people are less self-confident and more likely to ask and rely on advice from others. Unfortunately, they are also less likely to discern the quality of the advice or to recognize conflict of interest (Gino, Brooks, and Schweitzer 2012).

Moreover, fear of being perceived negatively up the organizational chain can prevent employees from communicating freely, offering feedback, or raising concerns due to the "fear of being viewed or labeled negatively, and as a consequence, damaging valued relationships" (Milliken, Morrison, and Hewlin 2003).

Managers are also afraid of negative feedback, and their perceived assumptions about employees can also further cut down on their desire to share information, which creates a culture of silence and stifles innovation (Morrison and Milliken 2000).

It is not a surprise that these are such strong forces: The fear of social ostracism is actually wired in our brains—a team of researchers from UCLA found that social exclusion fires up the same parts of our brains that detect physical pain (Eisenberger, Lieberman, and Williams 2003).

Unfortunately, communication breakdowns can lead to decreased trust. In fact, a recent survey shows that employees do not trust their organizations, with one in three surveyed reporting that their employer isn't always honest and truthful with them. "This lack of trust should serve as a wake-up call for employers," said David W. Ballard, PsyD, MBA, who is head of APA's Center for Organizational Excellence. "Trust plays an important role in the workplace and affects employees' well-being and job performance" (Excellence 2014).

We have seen the lack of transparency fuel fear within organizations, especially in times of change. I will never forget a full-day session I led for the leadership team of a major airline right after the announcement of a merger. The fear was palpable, but what the leader of the team did masterfully was to share as much information as she could at the time and very authentically say that there were still a lot of unknowns, including the future of her own role. Sometimes being present and transparent as a leader, even if you don't have all the answers, can do wonders for the culture of a team in the midst of turmoil.

On the micro level, I recognize the effects of fear on my own behavior. For every story I have for when our team has been hitting on all cylinders and is really in the mindset of discovery, I have just as many about the mindset of fear—especially about myself.

The mindset of fear has actually taught me more about the relationship between mindset and actions than I care to admit. After years of self-observation, it becomes very obvious to me if I am behaving in an unproductive way that does not create a positive environment for our team—and it's almost always due to the fact that I am deeply entrenched in the mindset of fear. This produces decisions and attitudes which then lead to bad conduct, such as focusing too heavily on the negative, not accepting the ideas of newer teammates, and deciding to do everything myself. It is also extremely predictable that the deeper I am in the mindset of fear the worse I will be.

The two biggest fears I've had as owner of the nation's longest-running comedy theater are:

1. Will I be perceived as a thoughtful and successful caretaker of the theater that Jenni and I bought and that was run by its founder for 39 years?
2. Will the company I am in charge of be able to financially support its employees?

One of the things that I dislike most about the mindset of fear is that it produces actions that can be completely contrary to one's actual intentions and aspirations. When I am being my most authentic self, I care deeply for both the institution I have been given the privilege to run and the wonderful people that I get to work with. However, the ironic thing about operating according to a mindset of fear—specifically, fear of failing in my role as leader—is that it causes me to act in ways completely contrary to what I actually care about. Said another way: It still amazes me that when I am in a mindset of fear I can act like such a jerk to the people I work with and care about deeply. Fear can take the best intentions and most heartfelt beliefs and twist them into desperate and confusing actions.

Such a discrepancy between our intentions and values and our behavior can be explained by the profound impact that stress has on our neurology. When under stress or when fearful, our brains are flooded by stress hormones such as cortisol and adrenalin. The frontal lobe, where most of our executive functions reside, shuts down and we lose our capacity for compassion, strategy, and trust building and we're left with more primitive responses such as fight, flight, appease, or freeze (Goldsmith 2014).

Effects can be lasting (Wellman, Brown, and Henning 2005). As Dr. Carla Wellman points out: "Exposure to stress—either over the long term, such as three weeks or even one week or just one day—can produce structural changes in the neurons of the prefrontal cortex. A neuron's shape is critically important to the way it processes information. We have seen profound changes as a result of stress and changes in behavior that the prefrontal cortex is directly responsible for" (Piurek 2008).

The good news, however, is that we may have more power over our stress responses than conventional wisdom dictates. There is a growing field of research on how *our perception* of stress is what determines whether stress will have a negative effect on our health and well-being. As Dr. Kelly McGonigal shared in a recent radio interview, stress is by definition rooted in our appraisals of a situation and *our perception* of our ability to handle it, the amount of support we may have, and in general our thoughts, feelings, and mindset (McGonigal 2015). In fact, according to McGonigal, we can respond to stress in ways other than fight-or-flight, which can be beneficial to us. These include a challenge response, which assumes we can do something about the situation to change it, and a *tend-and-befriend* response, which takes into account taking care of others and building community.

It's clear that stress and fear are significant factors in work productivity and the quality of relationships and interactions. We believe that teaching people to respond to stress and fear in a way that moves them forward, keeps them productive, and strengthens their relationships is a key factor that has to be addressed to create the innovation-friendly workplace of the twenty-first century. The truth is that our lives will continue to present us with circumstances that can trigger stress or fear; we don't believe it is realistic to say that we can avoid these experiences. However, the mindset through which we view them and the behaviors that we employ as a result are keys to our well-being and the success of our organizations. We are excited to provide strategies for transforming fear in the next chapters and empowering you to choose a mindset that helps you live a life of innovation and discovery.

The Symptoms of Fear

Although I see many of my own fear-based symptoms and behaviors in the clients we work with, I also see larger and more systematized ways fear has an effect on innovation efforts.

Some are common and easy to understand:

- When an organization asks people to embrace a sense of frugality and expense reduction, I often see people fearfully translate that into drastically decreasing the number of ideas they produce—because they could cost money.
- Sometimes I see leaders accidentally condemn the past when their intention is simply to energize and celebrate the future. That sometimes can affect the people they lead into thinking that all of their previous hard work wasn't innovative.
- There's the old standby that since the ultimate metric of whether or not our innovation was good or bad will be its return on investment, we should simply not waste any time considering ideas or innovations that won't make us money. That approach often blinds

us to the benefits of the idea not associated with ROI, which could be very profitable in another form.

■ Many groups are frightened to learn what a truly different and perhaps conflicting set of ideas will do to their innovation. They simply dub themselves content experts, which allows them to be insulated from something that could drastically change their path or strategy. Voice of the customer (VOC) is a prime example of how listening to an outside perspective can help innovation.

There are also some more subtle forms of fear that hinder good innovation:

We can get so enamored with the most popular or clearly commendable types of ideas—such as the equivalent of the next iPhone or other brand-new, disruptive products—that we can forget that there are many innovations that can help our organizations immensely, even though they're not as sexy. Some examples include great cost-reduction strategies, operational efficiencies, new partnerships, or even things we're *not* going to do anymore.

There are a few ways that fear commonly impacts behavior on the individual level:

■ The *Fear of Judgment*, or the What-If-I-Lose-Status Fret, often fuels a tendency to not do anything that stands out or to cover up one's unique point of view. People who are constantly qualifying their ideas or opinions or who are unwilling to share their full selves could be experiencing this fear.

■ The *Fear of Conflict*, or the What-If-I-Am-Not-Liked Fret, can cause apprehension when people anticipate resistance or tension related to their views or true opinions. We see this in people who change their minds, soften their opinions, or do not speak their truths when they expect conflict. It might also include people who keep quiet even though they disagree or see a different alternative.

■ The *Fear of Change*, or the What-If-I-Am-Not-Prepared Fret, can result in an impulse to resist change. We all experience a high degree of change nowadays and as a result are perhaps becoming more used to it. Yet there are still many of us who attempt to control our world and keep it neat and tidy by making lists and planning without end.

- The *Fear of the Unknown*, or the What-If-I-Am-Not-As-Smart-As-I-Thought Fret, can show itself in negative reactions from people who are presented with ideas or insights that are contrary to their opinions and beliefs or perhaps too out there and not in their frames of reference. That fear can also cause people to dismiss or attack their own or others' ideas or withdraw attention and avoid those ideas, opinions, or insights.

- The *Fear of Mistakes*, or the What-If-I-Am-Not-Perfect Fret, feeds off the desire for perfection and presents itself as a tendency to overthink, overanalyze, and overprepare all the time. Taken to an extreme, this fear shows itself in the face of a perfectionist who hesitates to act or experiences unhealthy, unproductive emotions when things don't go as expected.

The symptoms of all of these fears can wriggle their way into our behaviors and decisions in countless ways. Everyone knows what it's like when you're in a conference room and you come up with an idea and people say no. That's fear.

Harken Health's Ryan Armbruster, whom we met in Chapter 1, has told me he usually feels fortunate to be in environments in which he's working with people who are in the right mindset. But he shared one situation of a few years ago in which he pushed boundaries at one of the organizations he consults with.

Ryan: I tried to tackle some big issues and pointed my finger and said, "Gee, the healthcare system is not addressing the symptoms; we're at the bottom of a waterfall. By the time we're trying to help people, they're already in a bad position. What we'd really like to do is to help people stay healthy and not get into those bad positions."

John: This was well before the holistic approach to healthcare started to gain steam.

Ryan: Right. I put some progressive proposals on the table, and after the meeting, a participant referred to me as a socialist. Apparently I was pushing the boundary a little bit beyond someone's comfort zone, which is okay with me. I probably went right up to the edge on that one.

John: That's the mindset of fear talking.

Ryan: Interestingly enough, several years later, that initiative became a major strategic initiative.

John: I love how time does that. Your idea was: Couldn't we save money if we invested more in preventative care and good health? That was provocative then, and ultimately, that's what's going to have to happen, right? There is no way we're ever going to be able to afford everything, especially with the boomers. Yep, we'll just keep fixing them. The car keeps breaking so just bring it into the repair shop. There's no way we'll ever be able to afford that. It was supposedly socialist back then, but will it be common sense in a decade?

Ryan: Likely. It already is, somewhat—we are just behind in making the proper adjustments to a massive system. Also, many businesses that you and I both work with are often risk averse and not very open to innovation. Reliability and consistency is comfortable, but it also can be blinding.

There is a level of ambiguity in innovation. There is a level of risk. You can be really smart about it and that's really important, but it takes a little more dexterity than many organizations are designed to tolerate.

John: Got you.

Ryan: It's a level of comfort that you've got to try to get to. It's not a level of comfort with wasting money. It's just getting a little more comfortable with ambiguity and fine-tuning what you learn over time to generate success.

Last week I trained a group of high-potential leaders from an insurance company—all risk managers and actuaries. In this discussion about fear, they just wouldn't say the words. They'd just say, "We're not scared, we're just really financially prudent and really solid in our actuarial prediction of risk. We're not risk-averse. We just know what the numbers are."

But that's exactly what fear is.

6

The Anatomy of the Mindset of Discovery

Demi
Hey, I saw you in the cafeteria, you seem distracted or bummed? Everything okay?

Margi
Sorry, the marketing expo in Vegas is next week and I am just dreading it!

Demi
I thought you had retired from that thing?

Margi
So did I, but then Hopkins said she needed me to do it since I was the only one left from the team that did it last year.

Demi
Sorry to hear.

Margi
I just hate trade shows!!! The whole concept makes my skin crawl.

Demi
Me too, the carnival barking!

Margi
The cheesy giveaways!

Demi
The awkward booth-walking tote-bag fillers!

Margi
The forced networking!

Demi
Yuck.

Margi
And I have done *everything* I can to try and make it less than horrible. I spent extra for a large table, I have a flat screen for our brand video, I am giving away candy, and we hired an improv actor to engage the attendees when they walk by. Any other suggestions?

Demi
Do you have pens to give away? People love pens.

Margi
Yep, I Googled 10 things to make a trade show booth stand out, I even bought a new fishbowl for business cards.

Demi
Sounds like you have thought of it all, I am not sure what else you could change?

Margi
That's exactly what has got me down, I just hate it when there is nothing you can do to make a situation better. You know, when you are trapped and you just have to convince your mind to accept that this is going to be horrible but it will be over in a week.

Demi
Maybe if you book yourself a spa day to recover?

Margi
I wish I had the time!

O ne of the great blessings in my life is that the person who most often and most clearly demonstrates the mindset of discovery to me also happens to be my best friend and wife. Jenni seems to migrate to, sustain, and most naturally exist in this mindset. There are many days when I am sincerely jealous of what seems to be her effortless ability to approach life this way. Although Jenni works very hard at practicing and staying innovatively fit, being in the mindset of discovery seems to be almost her natural state.

The same isn't true for me. I remember a specific example of how her mindset choice blew me away.

In a relatively short amount of time, we had gotten the following news as a couple and as business owners:

- The two gentlemen who had co-directed and run our school of improvisation for five years were both leaving to take corporate jobs—at the same time.
- The building that had originally housed our theater (which we relocated in 2011) for almost 50 years and, after that, our school, was going to be sold, and we would need to move out within months.

This news came right on the heels of Jenni completing a miraculous journey of amazing hard work, innovation, and passion as she co-founded, chaired the board of directors, raised $5 million, bought and refurbished a building, hired an executive director and staff, and opened the doors of Gilda's Club Twin Cities, a free-of-charge drop-in clubhouse for anyone who has cancer or is connected to someone on the cancer journey.

It had been an exhausting period in her life and she truly was ready for a break—or at least a sabbatical from working and being a full-time mother to our two boys. But instead of getting to celebrate and enjoy all the successes she had had, she immediately had to get back into entrepreneur mode and:

1. Come out of retirement to be the school director (a position she had held from 1997 to 2003).
2. Find and hire replacements for our two co-directors.
3. Help me determine what kind of facility would best suit our school's needs for future growth.
4. Work with me to find and purchase such a facility.
5. Design the new space in a way that would make it accessible to our students and technically available to the rest of the world (through webcasts and distance learning).
6. Create a new train-the-trainer program to bring our improvisational curriculum well beyond our physical school.
7. Revamp the curriculum of our improv program.
8. Hire new teachers.
9. Create a new marketing plan for the school and its new approach and demographics.
10. Help me manage the construction process and equipment purchases.

Jenni accomplished all of that—and she did it within a year. The only thing that is more amazing than the actual accomplishment (which I completely attribute to her mindset) was the grace that she demonstrated and the positive culture she created for everyone involved in the project.

Jenni would be the first to tell you that the mindset of discovery is what allows her to take on these types of life challenges with a smile—and accomplish the seemingly impossible under circumstances that would prompt most people to quit.

I remember having a conversation with her when we realized what lay in front of us and all that we needed to do in the next year. I was overwhelmed, but Jenni said things like, "The undeniable drop-dead dates and urgencies will really help us to reduce any hesitation or over-analysis," "I'm sure when we look back on this year, we will be grateful for it to have been such a pivotal and explosive period in our company's history," and "I learned so much from the process of building Gilda's Club; it will be great to use that experience and knowledge right away on this other project, before I forget."

A mindset like this compels Jenni to behave consistently through highs and lows, to recognize possibilities, to listen for all available lessons, and to move forward into the unknown with a rational sense of risk and a miraculous sense of hope.

Most of us—including me—are far removed from spending as much time in the mindset of discovery as Jenni does. Think about how many minutes of your day you spend worrying about making a mistake at work, stressing out about workplace politics, checking out of superficial meetings, or overplanning and analyzing without taking action. Chances are various stressful thoughts, fears, and unhealthy judgments pop up in your head multiple times a day and take away from your energy and productivity.

We have found in our 15 years of working with businesses that in order to keep these stressors at bay, we have to be intentional about where we *focus our attention* and *what lens* we use to process information. We like to think of that filter as our mindset.

As psychologist and researcher Carol Dweck brilliantly points out in her book, *Mindset: The New Psychology of Success*: "Mindsets are just beliefs. They are powerful beliefs, but they're just something in your mind, and you can change your mind" (Dweck 2008).

We embrace a few powerful assumptions when we're in the mindset of discovery; specifically, we believe that:

- Mistakes are a great source of inspiration and learning.
- Change is fuel—not an obstacle.
- Ideas and honest opinions have value that we should celebrate, not judge.
- We all have the power to create change and impact those around us.
- We don't need *all* the information just to begin.

These assumptions fuel a very productive and happier state of being. We tend to be much more confident, agile, curious, accountable, and authentic when we're operating in the mindset of discovery.

The *confidence* stems from a healthy relationship with risk and alleged failure. It's easy to succumb to the fear of failure and attempt to spend disproportionate time on preventing mistakes and ensuring everything is perfect. No one likes to be wrong—and we aren't advocating a careless or fly-by-the-seat-of-your-pants approach. But mistakes will inevitably take place—and the people who are able to focus on learning and moving on are in a better place to keep trying to achieve their goals instead of giving up (Dweck 2008). They're more likely to take risks with confidence, because they know that they will learn something from the experience, regardless of the outcome.

The *agility* is rooted in the belief that irrelevance and stagnation follow if we don't change and grow. It replaces the belief that we won't be capable or competent on the other side of change with the assumption that change is fuel that *propels* the next stage, full of opportunity. People in the mindset of discovery don't seem to be set back or even surprised by change. They see the next circumstance in their life as simply a piece of information, and defer judgment on it in order to process it and find how it can help them move forward. This agility certainly has assisted the Brave New Workshop in its growth from a single entity of a theater to its current diverse set of product offerings and revenue streams, which include the theater, school, event center, and corporate training division. In each of those growth instances we responded to the opportunity that change can bring, instead of considering the changes obstacles or dead ends.

The *curiosity* is based upon a sense of openness—a desire to gather a wide breadth of information, perspectives, and experiences. It's not a passive level of curiosity; rather, it's an aggressive, investigative, almost inexhaustible need to learn, find out, and experiment. That curiosity shows itself in how people with it communicate with others, as well as in their ability to jump in and engage with a situation—or, in the context of innovation, begin to try things out. We'll talk more about how curiosity fuels our ability to listen, an important tenet in the mindset of discovery, later in the book.

The *accountability* is a manifestation of the desire to co-create and a belief that one has the power and ability to make an impact. Moreover, it's rooted in the capacity to see conflict as a productive process, which can lead to a better outcome. People in the mindset of discovery are not afraid to engage and mix it up if need be. They know that the friction of ideas, opinions, and points of view doesn't have to be full of contempt and negativity, and prefer to be active. They prefer to be doers and contributors rather than passive observers—or worse yet, self-appointed victims of circumstance.

Finally, the *authenticity* is a refusal to conform—and a celebration of diversity and a bold declaration of one's point of view, values, and opinions. Authenticity rests on the assumption that diversity of thought is the key to finding better solutions as well as creating a rich, interesting society and that pretending to be someone else does not serve anyone.

Mindset of Discovery = Foundation for Innovation

Many definitions of innovation exist, and for the purposes of this book we have embraced the definition cited in the *Oslo Manual* prepared by the Organisation for Economic Co-operation and Development and Eurostat, which has been adopted by the National Science Foundation Business R&D and Innovation Survey (BRDIS) (Boroush 2010): "Innovation is the implementation of a new or significantly improved product (good or service) or process, a new marketing method, or a new organisational method in business practices, workplace organization, or external relations" (Eurostat 2005).

This definition works for us because it includes the notion of creating *and implementing* something new and useful. Indeed, innovation is about thinking in new and different ways (creativity) as well as about making those ideas a reality (collaborating, socializing a concept, influencing, being a change agent).

A mindset of discovery is critical in the work of innovation because of its foundational importance.

We're all familiar with the learning pyramid model of tool sets, skill sets, and mindsets—with the last element being what everything else rests on top of. The proper mindset allows us to use the skills that we have developed and the tools that we are afforded in the specific ways we need them to accomplish tasks.

Salespeople, for example, need great product marketing collateral and the specific skills of value proposition articulation and closing.

However, what they need most of all is a foundational mindset of confidence, resilience, curiosity, and diligence. Even if salespeople have great tools and great skills, they won't achieve the results they're seeking if those tools and skills are set on top of a weak mindset—let alone one based on fear. The same goes for leadership, customer service, and especially innovation.

The great innovators I have encountered in my long career have had access to great tools and are certainly very skilled at ideation techniques, prototyping, finding disparate connections among ideas, or embracing odd, currently misunderstood concepts or premises. But mostly, they've embraced a discovery-based life approach and an innovative mindset.

Conversely, I know and have collaborated with thousands of people who might indeed have great tools and perhaps even great skills. However, when their foundation—their behavioral bedrock—is grounded in fear and not in discovery it's impossible for them to be great innovators. I've witnessed their frustrations with this phenomenon; some have asked me straight out, "Why is it that I work so hard at this formulaic approach to innovation or at this specific set of innovator tools and skills and yet my results don't seem to be as nearly innovative as I'd hoped?" As kindly as possible, I try to let them know that the answer is not more tools or skills, and that the way they see things must shift. It's their core approach that needs to be changed. They're never happy to hear that. It's personal, it's not a quick fix, and it's really, really hard.

The tool sets and skill sets are only part of the puzzle. It's that third leg of the stool—mindset—that's essential.

Kevin Wilde agrees. After more than 17 years he retired recently from his post as chief learning officer at General Mills, where he was responsible for the not exactly small area of personnel and organizational growth, including talent management and executive development. Kevin continues to share what he's learned through teaching, writing, and coaching. He serves as an executive leadership fellow at the Carlson School of Management, University of Minnesota, writes for *Talent Management* magazine, and contributes to a variety of books and publications.

Kevin is a lifelong friend and would certainly be considered one of the first significant executives to embrace what we were doing. Although perhaps risky at the time, Kevin took a chance in exploring this premise of improvisational behaviors in the workplace. He has helped shape and mold our application of improvisation to the workplace, and his early adoption was a significant boost to our approach and gave us validity in the eyes of many other organizations.

Kevin and I sat down to talk about the importance of all three elements—and fat suits.

John: Tool sets, skill sets, and mindsets, I'd love to hear your take on how those three important elements all work together.

Kevin: This notion about all three gives you a leveraged advantage versus just going after one of them. It's a popular topic in HR right now. Everyone's trying to transform their performance management systems. Typically, they're really after tools and techniques and skills. But I urge them not to forget about how important mindset is. And anytime you're trying to change something, think of a contribution you're making to mindset. I am a big fan of continued investments into being intentional and doing all the right cultural things that support where you're headed.

John: I believe that mindset can serve as kind of the bedrock upon which you build the skills and with which you use the tools. It has to come from the culture. You can have great tools and even specific skills, but if the mindset isn't there it's not as effective.

Kevin: Here's an example: A few years ago one of our innovation teams was trying to get our marketing managers to think about consumers who are trying to improve their health by losing weight. Every week or two they would assemble these business leaders, and they'd try diets out. So this week, they'd be on the Atkins diet, next week they'd be on the South Beach diet—all the diets consumers were trying. Most people got a real mindset shift of, "Oh, this is hard." But there was one guy—a thin, skinny guy who clearly never had to diet—who didn't understand how difficult it could be for people. Every diet he tried, he thought, "Yeah, fine, no problem." So finally they decided for the sake of consumer empathy that they would put him in one of these—I don't know if there's a delicate word for it—but a fat suit, with makeup and everything. His job was to live that life for a day, and so they assigned him to go shopping, go to McDonald's, go grocery shopping, and just experience what it's like being at a weight that you don't want to be.

That, finally, gave him the mindset. He became a great champion of empathy for that consumer based on that experience for that day. And because of that, he came up with and championed some very innovative products.

It wasn't just about attending a workshop and picking up tools and skills. He wasn't getting the mindset he needed to be in. Things clicked for him when he got into the mind of that consumer. In the consumer-foods business, you may be creating products that aren't your lifestyle but are someone else's. And you have to really understand that and really have empathy for that.

John: Empathy is a huge part of getting in the mindset of discovery. All the data in the world isn't worth a thing if you don't embrace the human element. You wouldn't be able to ever convince me that if I sit down and have coffee with someone and I get a feeling that he's sad or something, that that isn't a real, identifiable piece of energy. I'm actually pretty in tune with how emotions affect my body. Maybe it's because of improv, but I can be with someone for 30 seconds and tell you what my gut says about how he is.

Do you think that people can get better at that? Obviously, I'm biased toward that approach; but if it's essential for us to be able to gather that human information, can we practice it? And I guess, go out to coffee more, right?

Kevin: I'm biased, too, because I was a chief learning officer, so I inherently believe that you can get people to learn. I'm optimistic there. I would say the two conditions are (1) some people are wired for this more than others, and (2) some people have had more experiences than others. Given that, I think everybody can improve. Know that some cases are going to be easier, some cases are going to be harder, and there are some better ways of doing it; but yes, I do think that these areas are ones that you can grow.

Another reason why the mindset of discovery is so important in the work of innovation is its implications for creativity.

Creativity—or the *production of something novel and useful* (Jung, Mead, Carrasco, and Flores 2013)—provides the ideas and insights used to develop new or significantly improved products, processes, and methods. It's a vast area of study that has been of interest to humans since ancient times. New technology has most recently allowed researchers to begin to identify the brain processes and structures that are involved in it and to shed more light on how it emerges. While there are still many unknowns, evidence points to creativity as a combination of several cognitive processes instead of just one. Additionally, these processes don't rely on a specific region of the brain but rather brain networks and hubs, which are engaged at different times and for different purposes (Jung, Mead, Carrasco, and Flores 2013).

The brain networks necessary for creativity are different from those needed for intelligence. As neuropsychologist Rex Jung points out in an interview, intelligence requires strong and direct neural connections between networks, which provide fast information processing. Creativity, on the other hand, requires looser neural connections, which allow the brain to meander, helping us link unexpected ideas and concepts (Jung 2013).

The old myth of right-brain versus left-brain predominance is in fact incorrect. Cognitive processes, both analytical and creative, depend on the neural networks of the brain and use the whole brain, not just one part of it (Anderson, Nielsen, Zielinski, Ferguson, and Lainhart 2013).

The fact is, most of us don't exercise our creative brain networks on a daily basis—sometimes hiding behind the excuse that "I am not a creative or right-brained person." We rely on our intelligence and ability to recall or file information quickly, break down problems, and solve them as quickly as possible based on prior experience.

So it's no surprise that when we're in the innovation trenches, our biggest foe can be a mindset that focuses us on what is known and comfortable. It seems that when the process or task at hand demands that we be innovative we have to be willing and able to step away from the quick solutions and predictable ways of so-called normal. With effort and practice, if we can enter the innovation activity already in the mindset of discovery, preexisting fears, the status quo, and past failures can't affect our game. Mindset seems to be the most effective and all-encompassing way that I've seen to position ourselves for innovation success.

In the last few years, our company has done a significant amount of research and exploration into the science behind the innovative mindset. It revealed a huge bias on my part, perhaps because of my background or perhaps because of the fact that I *do* practice the mindset of discovery or because of the very nature of being an improviser. I always contended that people who weren't comfortable with risk—those who use *no* as their default answer or those who aren't willing to explore a point of view different from their own—were simply lazy. I was not aware of the many reasons why some people naturally migrate to the mindset of fear.

This research has proven to me that if we're not aggressively practicing and working on staying in the mindset of discovery, there's a more-than-likely chance that we'll passively and gradually—but just as consistently—migrate to the mindset of fear. My point of view has transformed from "it can certainly help you be more innovative" to "it's hard to ever be innovative without it."

So if consistently staying in the mindset of discovery is truly essential and an amazing accelerator to personal and cultural innovation, why don't people simply *choose* that mindset? After observing humans move in and out of this mindset for 15 years in my training sessions and talking to our clients about the difference between highly innovative groups and business as usual, we have uncovered one very potent reason why people don't remain in a mindset of discovery:

Because it's uncomfortable.

When we know something will make us uncomfortable—even if it's something we also know will help improve us—we typically avoid it. A frequent example is the process of coaching or giving or receiving feedback. We all know it is a wonderful tool to help ourselves grow, or to help strengthen the skill sets of those we lead, and yet sometimes the personal nature of feedback and discomfort associated with it has us procrastinate or sometimes even avoid it. So it makes sense to me that innovation would be uncomfortable to us. Innovation asks us to jump into the unknown, to embrace risk as a friend, to somehow convince ourselves that failure is a positive step toward an innovative solution. Some of its core elements ask us to do the very opposite of what has kept our species alive and evolving since the beginning of time. What are we, crazy? Why would that type of behavior and any of those processes feel good or comfortable?

Getting Comfortable Being Uncomfortable

I've witnessed thousands of individuals and hundreds of organizations try to create systems and processes that not only streamline the innovation process but are designed to somehow make the individuals who are innovating feel more comfortable with being more innovative. I've always scratched my head with that one—because I see it a bit differently.

Isn't innovation—or acting innovatively—always going to be a bit messy? Aren't the essential behaviors and actions of innovation always going to make most people feel a bit squeamish or uncomfortable?

What if we spend the same amount of time and effort and money on simply helping people be more comfortable with being uncomfortable? I've often thought that trying to make innovation more comfortable through processes and systems is kind of like trying to get Lake Superior a bit warmer or more comfortable so more people will swim. The water is cold: get used to it and jump in!

What I can attest to, having witnessed the process thousands of times, is that we can all actually increase our comfort with being uncomfortable through practice.

It's not as complicated as one might think. What we do in our exercises and what I prescribe for myself and others is to simply engage in safe, controlled activities that make us feel mildly uncomfortable. For us at the Brave New Workshop, that's simple improvisational exercises that put us in situations of ambiguity, or possible vulnerability, or that require us to be a different version of ourselves than we usually are.

Outside of improvisation, these kinds of activities can include something as simple as having a conversation with someone you don't know, listening to music that you currently don't appreciate, trying a new type of food, actually dancing at a wedding, getting up and singing during karaoke, or giving a public presentation to your peers or friends. Whatever is accessible, whatever works for you—just find some things that slowly, gradually, but consistently put you in situations in which you are uncomfortable. Faster than any physical fitness program you have ever been involved in, and with instant rewards of "Hey, that wasn't so bad" or "Wow, I was much better at that than I thought I would be," you will become more comfortable being uncomfortable.

I once took a series of tests that were meant to rank my tendency and comfort level with risk. The results of the test said that I had a very, very high—and I'm sure in some people's opinion unhealthy, perhaps even dangerous—level of comfort with risk. When I asked the test facilitators if they could possibly chart my score against other groups or types of people they said yes, although they were hesitant to tell me the results out of a concern for upsetting me. I told them not to worry; I came from a family of risk-takers and had been associated with lots of types of people in my life. They very calmly and in a data-reinforced way explained to me that the only community of people who shared the same scores in their comfort with risk-taking with me was the habitually incarcerated. How comforting.

My strong tendency to take risks can therefore make it hard for me to understand why everyone doesn't want to grab every opportunity to get uncomfortable. Thankfully, Kevin Wilde adds some weighty, solid context to my approach and pushes back at my inherent need to seek the uncomfortable at any cost:

John: We often talk about how important it is to be comfortable being uncomfortable. In my experience, I think you can get better at it. I spent a lot of time in college volunteering at a camp for kids with special needs. I was really awkward that first week of freshman year. I felt uncomfortable. I hadn't been around a lot of kids with special needs before. But by the end of the fourth summer, I wasn't the least bit uncomfortable anymore. And it simply came out of practice and repetition.

Kevin: What caused you to put yourself in that environment to begin with, and then how did you stick with it?

John: It's because there was a need to serve someone else. There was an opportunity to serve and help, and if that can be stronger than the awkwardness or discomfort, then you can follow that. Let that pull you. Let that drive you. That's certainly what drove me to volunteer at that camp. And the reward was instant. The first day I met this great kid on the softball field, and the first thing he said to me is, "John, I'm slow, but you're fat." And I said, "We're going to get along really well." I instantly felt less uncomfortable. I couldn't stop coming back. The rewards were so wonderful.

Kevin: To put it in a business context—companies are wired to reduce risk while achieving objectives. If I had to boil down my 34 years of corporate life, it would be like this: Leaders say, "I need to get this done. How do I reduce the risk while I get it done?" I think there's a lot to that.

What *you're* saying is counterintuitive: "You've got to put yourself into risk to achieve your objective." I think there's a paradox, if not a balance, there. "I need to get uncomfortable, but within reason." But on the edge, right? Because you can go *too* far or you can get *too* comfortable. And so how you build that muscle and that skill, and part of it is a skill, and part of it is giving you the tools, but part of it is, "How do I generate that right mindset?"

John: Setting the boundaries of how much risk you're going to take actually is a good way to help people manage their fear of risk. Then they know the boundaries. "We're going to go swimming in Lake Superior in August, and the water's 61 degrees, so it's going to be pretty cold. You're going to shiver and it'll be a little painful for a while, but you're not going to get hypothermia. We're going to come out in five minutes and it's going to be okay."

In the work that I do I am still amazed that people will just say, "I'm sorry, I can't stand up and sing and dance in front of my peers. It's simply too much risk." Before we do exercises, I say: "Can we please identify the spectrum of consequences for what we're about to take risks on? No one will get a disease, no one will get shot, and no one will get fired."

I think we magnify how risk-tolerant we are or aren't. If you really feel uncomfortable doing something, that's the single biggest reason you should do it.

Kevin: While that's definitely true—it could be equally aimless to seek discomfort without aiming to achieve a purpose. I think what caused you to hang in there wasn't just, "Well, I'm comfortable being uncomfortable." You were also saying, "I'm trying to get a greater good done. I'm going to hang in there because I'm convinced this is going to help me get there."

John: Right—it's not just the carrot. It's the actual reward and things that you were able to get done. It's worth it. The journey's worth it, because we know the result.

Kevin: Every September, I take about 20 people on a day hike of the Grand Canyon. We start at one rim of the canyon and we take 12 hours, drop a mile into the canyon, cross the Colorado River, and then go up the other side. The whole thing is 24 miles. There are lots of signs from the National Park Service that say, "Don't do this in a day." We do it in a day.

John: Wow.

Kevin: I'm in one of the most stunningly beautiful places on Earth. You go through the ages and layers of the planet. For the most part, it's a four-foot-wide trail that just continues forever. But here's the interesting part: I have to remind myself to look at it. Because for the 12 hours that I'm doing this, I'm looking at my feet. I think back to why I'm taking the risk or why I'm being uncomfortable. I have to remind myself where I'm headed and why I'm doing this darn thing.

We get to the base of the canyon and it's 100 degrees. There are no taxis or buses; the only way out, other than emergency helicopter, is on your own two feet. And you get kind of grumpy about it. So you've got to remember to look up at why you're here in the first place—in the middle of that stress and frustration.

That experience reminds me of what you talked about regarding your summer camp. It wasn't just that you got uncomfortable; it's that you had a purpose.

John: In the business context—especially as a leader—that means being able to communicate to those people you're asking to hike with you into the canyon. You want them to continue to look up and then give them some great examples of what they're looking up for. This is how it's going to help profitability, help our customers, help our culture. It's not just for the sake of innovation or being uncomfortable.

I get pretty adamant about telling people, "You should push yourself and be uncomfortable just so you can be an uncomfortable athlete." But it has to be bigger than that, especially for people who don't necessarily like risk.

Kevin: Yeah. You can't get by on just being comfortable. I'm reminded of a quote that I think Napoleon was credited with saying: "A leader reminds people what's important." If it's important enough, you're willing to get uncomfortable. And I can't do it any other way.

I'm not only comfortable with being uncomfortable, I often pursue it. While this attitude isn't for everyone, I know that it's just how I am wired. I have also learned over the years that trying to be comfortable being uncomfortable is a very difficult thing for many wonderful and innovative people. So I have spent some time trying to develop ways to help them increase *their* ability to be comfortable being uncomfortable. I'll discuss some of those methods in this book; you can find others in other books and methodologies. One of the single most effective ways to get people to begin—though it's not glamorous and perhaps seems so obvious that it's embarrassing even to mention—is *to be in the service of others.*

I talked a little about service to others as it related to my summer camp experience in my conversation with Kevin. If we try to help, first and foremost—to improve the lives of another, come to the aid of someone in need—we tend not to notice or perhaps simply just ignore many of the "I'm about to be uncomfortable so I should stop what I'm doing" signals and alarms. It works like a distraction. I've never been able to—or met anyone who's been able to—simultaneously be completely engaged in serving another human being while at the same time worrying, fretting, or being preoccupied with personal discomfort.

As you heard earlier, my friend Sr. Laureen Virnig has lived most of her remarkable life in service to others. And as you might expect, she's got an amazing perspective on just how transformative that can be, particularly when the service takes the form of something that is practiced again and again.

John: Being in the service of others is as deep of a thread as anything in your life. Everything you do is for others in some ways.

Sr. Virnig: You know that saying, "If you throw mud on somebody else, part of it lands on you"? If you throw affirmations on others, part of it lands on you, too.

I remember when I had moved to a new city, I was probably in my early 20s. There was an expectation that we wouldn't go to our families at Christmastime. But I was lonely, so I said, "Oh heck, I'm going to go to the nursing home across the street." It was just a beautiful Christmas because I met those lonely people and they were so happy to see this little peanut coming over there.

John: And you got something out of it, also.

Sr. Virnig: If I give, something is coming back. It's like my mom used to say, "If you point fingers at somebody else, most of them are pointing back at you." And what I see in others often is what I see in myself. It's like when someone asks, "What are the people like in California?" And you answer, "Oh, they're just wonderful people." Well, *you* must be a wonderful person.

John: You clearly haven't met any of the Sweeneys of California. That's exactly it. If we reduce our judgment of others' ideas, our residual benefit may perhaps be that we're a little less judgmental of *our own* ideas. Because one of the biggest inhibitors of new ideas is that they never see the light of day as a result of our own judgment. A lot of our work is based on helping build corporate cultures, but we also teach people how to build their own personal innovation programs. That way when the idea comes they can at least be neutral. It is just an idea. And we don't have to beat it up.

Sr. Virnig: You don't have to judge it. Just get it all out.

John: And then it might combine with another idea, or, more beautifully, another person might *react to it*. That's why I'm so opposed to these process-driven innovation programs; they have algorithms judge the ideas and don't give another human the chance to say, "What that means to me is … "

Sr. Virnig: I think one of the images we have here, spoken or unspoken, is of everybody bringing a candlelight of wisdom to the decision: That my little light might be pretty dim—but if I get yours, our combined light is that much stronger. So we have all this feed in. That's when we get light—in the next step.

John: It seems to me that when you incorporate a habitual practice in your life—in this case, being of service to others—that you can find consistency in that practice. And when you do it for years and decades, it also surprises you with wondrous gifts of, wow, I didn't know this would happen. Have you had examples of there being these wonderful blessings and surprises that really are just a function of the small things that you do every day that show themselves?

Sr. Virnig: This is very minor, but I lost my keys. Do you ever do that?

John: Every day. I don't know where mine are right now. They're probably in the car.

Sr. Virnig: And I could just spend time looking for the keys and worrying about the keys, but there was something else that I was asked
to do. Somebody needed something and so I decided to just go do it.
The keys have to find me. I went to help this person and then that
led to me helping someone else with another project. She needed
help and I did that.

And I came back and my keys were where I had looked earlier.
I'm so sure I'd looked there. How was that possible? Everyone said,
"Oh, you just were looking over them." Well, that's just a small
thing, but sometimes just letting go of focusing on me, and instead
focusing on someone else's needs, is what makes all the difference.

John: So to your point—if I'm uncomfortable with this change in my
job or accepting a new idea, it's a nice distraction away from my
own issues if I can put myself in the service of others.

Sr. Virnig: With oblates, there are three key components: prayer,
community, and service. How am I part of the community? In
other words, who am I looking at? Well, service is in there, too.
Who am I looking at outside of myself? What can I give today?
What can I bring today? What is that saying? "Practice random
acts of kindness and senseless acts of beauty."

John: Sometimes it acts as such a wonderful angle or distraction. And
then we find the keys.

It's almost as if we put on special I'm-serving-others glasses that
block out the things that make us uncomfortable. There are countless
drastic examples, such as the Herculean efforts in life-or-death situations of average citizens who run into a dangerous situation to save
another person.

But the ones I tend to learn the most from are a bit simpler.
When we are silly and we pretend during playtime with a child, we're
never embarrassed—because we know our interaction is helping the
all-important brain development of that child *and* making her smile.
When grandma makes a horrible meal, we swallow and smile because
her sense of independence and dignity means much more to us than
the completely inappropriate overuse of garlic. When we volunteer
with communities who are much less fortunate than ours, we're so

overcome by their need and the need to serve, that many of the typical inconveniences or uncomfortable aspects of our lives go completely unnoticed (such as temperature, bugs, hygiene, and smells). If you or anyone you know has ever gone on a third-world medical mission, this phenomenon of the service distraction is everywhere in those wonderful endeavors.

The next time innovation needs you to be uncomfortable, remind yourself that your innovation is for the sake of others; it is to serve the solution and the solution may serve your customers and this world.

7

Building Your Innovation Fitness Plan

Declan
How's the training for the 5K coming?

Maygen
So-so, I'm finding it hard to make the time.

Declan
I hear ya, I haven't been to the gym in weeks.

Maygen
Yep, it's hard to commit time to it with all the other things going on.

Declan
Hey, did you see who won on *American Idol* last night?

Maygen
No, I was watching the last episode of *The Bachelor*.

Declan
Don't tell me, I TiVoed it and will watch it tonight.

Maygen
You will be shocked. I'm just finishing up the final episode of *Breaking Bad*—it's taken me months to get through the whole series.

Declan
I'm the same with *Mad Men*.

Maygen
Want to go for a run tomorrow?

Declan
Wish I could, way too busy.

I 've had the privilege of experiencing three dramatically different worlds throughout my life—competitive college sports, the performing arts, and business. One thing that has always stuck out for me is the difference in how the concept of practice is implemented in those three worlds. In sports and the arts, we tend to practice most of the time and execute far less frequently. For example, it was clear to me why we practiced five time a week for three hours for one game on Saturday, why when I changed positions on my college football team I had to spend countless hours practicing the specific skills that were needed to be successful in that new position, and why the specific weight-lifting regimen my coaches gave me was directly related to the muscles most important to my role.

In the world of theater, we spend 30 minutes warming up our voices, 30 minutes warming up our bodies, and 30 minutes warming up our minds to begin the daily *rehearsal* for the current show. Even improvisation, which is created on the spot, takes significant preparation and a robust warm-up to be executed successfully.

And then there's the world of business, which demands that we wake up, drink our cup of coffee, and execute, execute, execute all day long. When we are asked to improve, to learn new skills, and to meet our professional development goals, we hardly ever get the time or support necessary for meaningful practice. It still seems absurd to me that we have reviews only once a year—just one chance every 365 days to identify skillset gaps, to understand that we need to become better innovators, leaders, teammates. But then ... what? More often than not, we get back to work, or if we are lucky we receive a book, a PowerPoint presentation, perhaps a WebEx, and—if we are *extra* lucky—a day of training. Then it's business as usual, and the application of the skills and the practice of the foundational behaviors necessary to support the new skills are supposed to come naturally.

They hardly ever do.

For real improvement and meaningful behavioral changes we need a plan that's integrated into our daily lives. We need something that provides the opportunity to practice and reflect on the new skills and behaviors.

When it comes to innovation, we know that mindset and the behaviors it fuels are crucial for success. We also know that the mindset of fear—so prevalent in today's workplaces—hinders any innovation efforts. So how do we overcome our brain's wiring, our aversion to discomfort, and our learned behavior in order to foster a mindset of discovery?

Is it even possible to change our mindsets—or is the way we've been operating our whole lives engrained in us forever? *Yes*—we absolutely can change. Carol Dweck—a leading authority on the science of mindset—and her team have completed multiple studies that show that when students are taught a specific mindset called a *growth mindset*, they are able to adopt it and increase their academic performance (Dweck 2013). When armed with the right mindset, students are also able to build resilience for academic and social challenges (Yeager and Dweck 2012).

According to Dweck, one needs to do the following to change one's mindset (Dweck 2014):

1. *Recognize* mental patterns and the voice of the unproductive mindset.
2. *Reframe* information through the lens of the productive mindset.
3. *Choose* one's behavior.

If you don't know who Diana Shulla-Cose is—or anything about her work—you definitely should. She's as innovatively fit as they come, and a living, breathing example of Carol Dweck's growth mindset.

Diana and her colleague Kim Day founded Perspectives Charter Schools nearly 20 years ago in the basement of the Chicago public school where they were teaching. Perspectives is now a network of five public schools, all located on the south side of Chicago, covering sixth through twelfth grades. More than 90 percent of their students come from economically disadvantaged backgrounds.

They've developed an academic model that they call the Disciplined Life education model that merges two things: academically rigorous college-prep classroom learning and social-emotional learning. Schools, of course, are supposed to do the first part. We expect them to impart academic rigor and get kids prepared for college.

The other side of it, though, is where Diana's innovative mindset has taken root. Students at Perspectives spend almost 200 minutes a week in a class called A Disciplined Life® that focuses on social-emotional learning in a very intentional, focused way. It's a framework that they call SRP, which is built around self-perception, relationships, and productivity.

Diana was an easy choice to include as a profile in this book. We are friends for life; I have known her for more than 30 years and have watched her life journey from a hard-working and dedicated gifted athlete to a passionate young educator to a wonderful wife and mother who has literally reinvented education.

Everything about Diana's journey lies in the mindset of discovery. *Fearless* is almost always the first word that comes to mind when I think of her. Her passions about fulfilling others' needs completely eliminate hesitation. She is bold about her declarations regarding what it takes to get the important work she is doing done. There are no obstacles for her, simply the need to figure out new ways to accomplish what is needed.

Perhaps more than anyone I know, she's a person who often spurs reactions such as, "Wow, I can't believe she was able to do that." Or, "Holy cats, I don't think I would have had the guts to do what she just did." She stretches outside her comfort zone each and every day. The world that she lives in is miles away from the world that she came from. But like most innovation heroes, she took all of the wonderful things she was given in her past and uses them every day to solve problems, find solutions, and raise up those around her.

Diana's work has an exponential impact because it involves children. The thousands of lives that she has helped mold and improve will move on in life to affect thousands more. The 26 principles of

A Disciplined Life that her school embraces and that she helped to develop can teach each and every one of us how to be better people, leaders, and students of life.

John: Part of what we wanted to share with our readers is that even the most innovative people in the world—even the trailblazers like you—get scared and have doubts. We want readers to know that it's natural to question yourself, or not be completely sure if your ideas are the best, or doubt whether you're the right person for the job. We want them to know that everybody does that.

The question is: What do you do next? I believe that if people practice certain behaviors on a daily basis, they can transform their mindset into one of discovery. Let's talk about how you do it. You take a kid from a specific place, mindset, community, and culture. By having him practice these 26 principles of A Disciplined Life in a very regular and loving, yet disciplined way, you literally transform that child. That child is different when he graduates from Perspectives from when he started. How does that work?

Diana: First, I fully believe in the idea of the growth or discovery mindset. Perspectives believe that the 26 principles of A Disciplined Life can be taught. *Show Compassion* and *Love Who You Are* can be learned. So can *Show Gratitude* and *Think Critically* and *Be Inquisitive*. These are a few of our 26 principles that we teach to develop a discovery mindset that empowers new thinking, new expectations, and ultimately new outcomes. I'm inspired by Carol Dweck's brilliant work about teaching for the growth mindset versus the standard mindset. She talks about creating classrooms that encourage risk-taking and mistake-making. As lifelong learners we must see ourselves as risk-taking, mistake-making people with grit every day—we can, we will, end of story.

This kind of affirmation empowers kids to be learners. I would love to have had someone telling me that while I was growing up. If somebody came at me with that intention about mindset I would have been a different learner. It's critical that the exploration of mindset is surfacing in a very intentional way, not only for our young people but for innovators and leaders of communities and companies—because it's transformational.

John: Can you cite an example of how you're putting that into action at Perspectives?

Diana: One of our 26 principles is to *Solve Conflicts Peacefully*. Our students are taking our principles to the streets, and we're doing it through the lens of violence in our city. Our students have started the I Am for Peace movement. Our students need and deserve safe communities in which they too use the word *peace* to describe their front porches or backyards. Our students are fighting violence with the 26 principles of A Disciplined Life. We believe that we can build a more peaceful city. We may not end violence or stop the use of handguns, but we can know our role and play our part.

Brandy Woodard is the principal of our Perspectives Math and Science Academy. She addressed an ongoing incident between a handful of her teenage males and a handful of young men from a neighboring school. They were fighting after school near the train platform and were sustaining the bad energy between the two groups. The fighting grew worse and even involved the police at one point. Brandy *Took Initiative*, brought her boys together, and asked, "How do we model A Disciplined Life and solve this problem?"

Because of her leadership and the students' capacity for self-reflection and problem solving, they decided collectively that they wanted to meet with the young men from the neighboring school. Our students and staff created a space for this group of approximately 20 young men to get to know one another, have critical conversations about their problems, and find solutions together.

After three sessions of critical conversations about solving conflicts peacefully while playing video games and basketball together, they designed a button that included both school logos, representing their united front. They are also planning to march for peace together in June just as summer begins.

This powerful story illustrates how we apply our social-emotional learning curriculum. It's a real-life situation in which educators provide the forum and practice and students apply the tools they've learned. These young men have experienced the process of making change—they have moved from fights and fists to minds and hearts to solve problems. They know what change looks like and that the cycle of violence can be interrupted—because they did it! Schools must pay attention to this kind of learning—and they must do it now with thoughtful intention and high expectations and a lot of love.

John: Wow. Your Perspective boys would not have been able to come to the conclusion that they needed to go and take peaceful action and live these principles unless they had been practicing those principles for a long time, right?

Diana: Exactly. Not only practicing them and having them in their hands—but also being exposed to the forum in which to have those conversations. You can't necessarily take math class and history class and talk about these subjects on a weekly basis. Our 26 principles emerge in our daily classes as well as in so many other aspects of the school community. Living A Disciplined Life together is the mindset at Perspectives. Striving to embody them means a successful and meaningful life.

John: This social and emotional piece—maybe call it a mindset; call it whatever it is—but that part of a human being that you people are transforming, it's so important that, unlike other schools, you literally have carved out a significant amount of time in the classroom for it, which says: "This is as important as trigonometry, we need to be able to peacefully resolve conflict. We need to study and make these principles habitual so that when we're brawling with other kids, we know what to do because we've been educated in it."

Diana: Our students are evaluated on the 26 principles just as they are on algorithms in math and revolutions in history. That's what we do at Perspectives. Every semester, a student grapples with one principle in A Disciplined Life and then demonstrates what she has learned about it. If the student is studying the principle Take Responsibility for Your Actions, she collects data on how and when she took responsibility—and when perhaps she didn't—and looks at the repercussions of each.

John: And it's not just the kids.

Diana: Our teachers study the 26 principles, too. On every teacher's door there's a sign that says, "I'm studying the principle ... " that names whichever one it is. I'm studying the principle *Seek Wisdom* right now. Our 26 principles of A Disciplined Life permeate the culture of the entire family. It's not just a class—it's a culture and a language we use to guide our actions. Parents commit to studying principles every semester, side-by-side with their children. Our board members study the principles, too. At our annual benefit the other night, our board chair said, "I'm studying the principle *Show Gratitude.*" One of our funders said, "I'm studying the principle *Be a Lifelong Learner.*"

John: When you sit back and ask, "Why is my high school graduation rate better than double what the norm is," is it because the students at Perspectives learn both academics and social-emotional principles?

Diana: Perspectives graduates are different. When our graduates walk across the stage at 18 years old, they carry with them the tools to be successful, comprehensive, and deeply experienced social-emotional learners. They know how to self-manage, make thoughtful decisions, set goals, and persevere, and they know and show empathy. We teach both EQ (emotional quotient) and IQ at Perspectives—the whole child. We say that our graduates are young *ethical leaders.* There are leaders everywhere. But to put the word *ethical* in front of the word *leader* creates the kind of leaders that we need—in our homes, in our communities, and across the globe. Embodying the 26 principles is a lifetime of discovery. At Perspectives we're committed to striving to embody these every day, and ultimately we're going to change the world by doing it.

I remember visiting Diana's first Perspectives classroom. Never in my wildest dreams would I have believed that she—or anyone else, for that matter—could have taken that idea, that vision, that need to serve, and turned it into a $30-million-per-year multi-campus educational institution/miracle.

After our conversation, I couldn't help thinking about how many hundreds, and perhaps thousands, of times in the early stages of building this school, she and the other courageous pioneers of Perspectives could've been completely justified in quitting—and almost encouraged to. They were up against all of the same things that I hear about every day as obstacles to innovations in large organizations. No budget, no support from the top of the organizational chart, not enough time, not the right facilities, not enough personnel, not enough technology, sometimes not even the support of the very people they were trying to help.

But Diana and Kim didn't quit. They pushed on, continued to innovate, made do with what they had, and ignored what they couldn't do while putting laser focus, attention, and effort into what they could do.

The Perspectives model is the future of education in our country. For our entire American school system's history, we've focused solely on academics. This model has come along and essentially proven that the emotional and social aspect is important. Diana and her team said, "We're going to create a curriculum for it. We're going to teach it every day. We're going to test on it. And that is going to create a total human being who is going to be more innovative and more successful, and who is going to graduate and become an ethical leader."

That quantum leap from the old way of thinking in academics can be applied to the business world as well. The model of "We can't teach soft skills in corporations because we're too busy learning technical skills and learning sales skills and learning profitability skills" is completely outdated. The potential for improvement is enormous.

Breaking the Patterns

Diana relies upon and practices her school's 26 principles to keep innovatively fit. When it comes to our own individual innovation fitness plans, we've each got to identify our own metrics to say, "I'm staying in shape here; things are on the right track." How does that show up in your life? For me, I'll notice I just had a pretty cool conversation with someone that I absolutely disagree with, and that I must be doing okay because I didn't punch him. That's one of my key innovation fitness measurements: Can I appreciate diverse points of view in an authentic and real way?

Everybody has their own ways of measuring their innovation fitness. But one that many people share is looking at the degree to which we're avoiding the "We've always done it this way, so why not do it that way again?" way of thinking. That's an extremely common trap to fall into, and our brains are constantly pushing us in that direction, since it's often the easiest route to take.

Harken Health's Ryan Armbruster lives and breathes innovation, but even he gravitates toward defaulting to what's worked in the past:

John: You've said that sometimes a wealth of experience can actually work against you when it comes to innovation.

Ryan: Right. After 20 years in the healthcare industry, with at least 10 of that being spent full-time on innovation, you accumulate a lot of knowledge and experience. There are so many roads that I've been down before. One of my innovation fitness metrics is keeping track of how quickly I tune things out because I'm leveraging past experience. If I continually do that, I know that's not the right solution. But that's what we want to do, because we've already been down that road. We've tried that. We've done that. From a curiosity and innovation perspective that's exactly what blinds you.

It's a challenge. You don't want to spend a lot of time just rehashing, rethinking, redoing, redoing. You want to contribute to getting to the next step. I often have this huge conflict between: Do I really open my mind and rethink that right now, or do I just go back and leverage the experience I already have and say, okay, let's do it that way? We've got to move on to something else because I don't think we have potential there. It's tough.

John: Time pressure adds to that challenge, right? We say, "Well, I know I can get this done based on past experience, so maybe we'll just get it done that way instead of finding an innovative way to do it."

Ryan: Absolutely. Sometimes I don't like having that much experience to go back to. Sometimes I'd prefer to be the 27-year-old who's insanely curious and wants to challenge everything that's going on.

So how do we overcome our natural inclination to go back to that "it's always worked this way" well, especially if we've got multiple examples of doing it that way to refer to?

We've got to change our brains.

Changing our Brains

In Chapter 5 we discussed how the roots of fear connect with the way our brains have evolved. The great news is that overcoming fear is also a big part of the human experience; in fact it's an integral reason for our survival as a species. As Greg Downey, a professor of anthropology from Macquarie University, shares in a radio interview, human evolution depended on our ancestors overcoming fear. Doing so allowed them to become hunters and turn themselves into predators. This was due to the prominent executive function in our brains, which allows us to talk to ourselves and override the older parts of our brains (Downey 2015).

So the good news is that *overcoming* fear is just as human as experiencing it. We know that adult brains can change and improve. In the past 20 years the field of neuroscience has exploded and the concept of neuroplasticity, or the ability of the brain to change even in adult years, has been widely accepted. We now know that with practice we are actually able to change our brains and affect not only the gray matter where most processing happens, but also the white matter, which connects the different parts of the brain.

In a 2009 study, Oxford researcher Dr. Heidi Johansen-Berg and her team showed that after six weeks of juggling training (weekly training sessions and 30-minute practices each day) there were changes in the white matter of the test group compared to the others who had received no training. The changes were in regions of the brain that are involved in reaching and grasping in the periphery of vision (Scholz, Klein, Behrens, and Johansen-Berg 2009).

Aside from motor skills training, there is evidence that mental training also has profound impacts on the brain. A study conducted on participants in an eight-week meditation course showed decreased activity in the amygdala when viewing various emotionally charged images while not meditating. This is the first study to show the lasting effects of mental training. Interestingly enough, subjects who practiced compassion meditation showed spikes in amygdala activity in response to negative images—all of which depicted some form of human suffering (Desbordes et al. 2012).

Truly, we become what we practice as we strengthen the brain networks associated with the activities we are working on. And that makes those activities not only easier, but also more automatic.

Habit Transformation

Our habits can be another barrier to adopting the mindset of discovery and making innovation business-as-usual.

Habits are powerful. They serve a wonderful purpose—to save us time and brain energy. Indeed, if none of our behavior or thinking was automated we would be spending our days just trying to navigate the most common everyday tasks. Once we've mastered an activity through repetition, it becomes automatic—allowing us to focus on more challenging or creative work.

The downside occurs when we form unproductive or harmful habits that no longer fit with our goals. These can be hard to change. The challenge comes from the very nature of habits: They are subconscious and triggered by cues in our environment (Dean 2013).

Behaviors rooted in fear are therefore usually habitual—making them all the more challenging to transform. But time, dedication, and an intentional plan can help us avoid them.

Getting rid of a bad habit can be tricky, too, because you can never truly extinguish bad habits (Duhigg 2012). The way to manage them is to study their mechanics—the cue that triggers the habit, the routine (what the habit is), and the reward that we get by performing the habit. Then, and only then, can we replace the routine with a new, more productive behavior, which should be triggered by the same cue and should provide the same reward.

Learning from and connecting with other people in order to build productive habits can often pay huge dividends. Gina Valenti is one example of someone who credits her partners, coaches, bosses, and mentors with helping her take full advantage of the opportunities presented to her—and helping her become more innovative in the process:

John: You've got lots of stories about positive personal transformations that have happened within the Hampton team, in which someone started in one role and learned and grew and was courageous, and then went to another role and another role. That's true about the entire brand, and I think it's because the team also has to live Hamptonality.

Your own story's great. You're a swimmer. You're an athlete. You started working at a hotel. There are these things about this service that you love, and, next thing you know, you're head of culture and brand for Hampton. How? You've had a career of transformation and growth that's courageous and full of innovation, and I just want to hear your voice on how people can practice and grow.

Gina: I think it's a couple of things, and thank you for the kind words. I really will put that all back on my boss, Phil Cordell, because he's the one that saw the opportunity. He saw the opportunity when Hampton was starting to swim in a sea of sameness, and he asked how do we differentiate Hampton? We have a great product, but it's really easy to copy product. So we have to focus on the people and culture.

Working with a leader that you admire, trust, and respect will unleash the best in you. What Phil did is he trusted me. He empowered me. He enabled me. There wasn't a culture department anywhere within our company. It was back in 2005 when culture wasn't the buzzword. He saw that as an opportunity and he saw my passion for people, and he really trusted me.

Having a leader who has a vision that gives me hope and who allows me to use the best of me, who identifies my strengths and then lets me use them to contribute, that's been key.

The other piece is the line of coaches and mentors I have. They are all great thought partners. The ability to be able to reach out to someone like John Sweeney and say, "Hey, I have this problem that needs to be solved. I don't know how to do it, and you're way cleverer, so let's think about this!"

Somebody finally gave me a big sign for my home that says, "I get by with a little help from my friends." The only problem with that sign is it should say, "I get by with a lot of help from my friends," because I really lean into people that are smarter and more fun. It takes a village, and my village is filled with savvy, thoughtful, and innovative thought leaders who have become my friends over the years. We often say, "Let's make great together." That's a lot of fun for me. I don't think I could exist without my boss and my thought partners.

Let's Begin!

Research shows that our habits can put our intentions at odds with our behaviors. If a habit is strong, we are less likely to act according to our intention if it is contrary to the habit. If a habit is weak, however, we have a better chance of acting according to the intention (Dean 2013). A strong habit is qualified as something we do at least once a week as part of our everyday behavior. A weak habit is a once-in-a-while activity. Participating in your company's charitable-giving campaign once a year would be a weak habit, but checking your e-mail on your phone first thing after you wake up would be a strong habit. With that in mind, when we go about transforming our mindsets and becoming more innovative, it is not enough to simply *decide* to be in the mindset of discovery.

Having a strong motivation and a goal in mind is important, however; if you are hoping to change the way you approach your daily work and life, chances are you are dealing with strong habits. This will require you to create a detailed plan of how you will *behave* in various situations to ensure that you reinforce new behaviors, which will increase your innovation fitness.

The next chapters will examine five behaviors that we believe can replace some more common fear-based behaviors and increase the time we spend in the mindset of discovery. Those simple yet powerful behaviors—which we call the Big Five—are:

1. *Listen*: Be present, open, and aware.
2. *Defer judgment*: Pause and accept the potential of ideas and opinions.
3. *Declare*: Be authentic and clear, speak your mind.
4. *Reframe*: Use what you have to move forward.
5. *Jump in*: Develop a bias toward action, avoid analysis paralysis.

We'll help you create your innovation fitness plan by providing you with sample scenarios of how to intentionally practice each behavior, a deconstruction of the behavior's components, examples of what the behavior looks like in real life, why the behavior is important to innovation, and tactics that can help you incorporate that behavior into your daily routine.

Let's jump in.

8

Listening

Alejandro
How did your review go?

Yvette
So-so. I'm not sure if he really heard me.

Alejandro
How so?

Yvette
I told him that I felt like I was reaching a burnout level in my current assignment.

Alejandro
What did he say?

Yvette
He said that it's typical for a career path to have cyclical fluidity.

Alejandro
What did you say?

Yvette
I said that I didn't think the team was working well together.

Alejandro
What did he say?

Yvette
He said that a healthy level of cross-silo positive friction was a good ingredient for human capital maximization.

Alejandro
What did you say?

Yvette
I said it was my birthday.

Alejandro
What did he say?

Yvette
He asked if I had filled out the online engagement survey and if I had completed the HR and Compliance e-learning modules.

Alejandro
So what makes you think he wasn't listening?

There's a reason that listening is the first of the Big Five behaviors we cover. It's perhaps the most important, and it's also the one that seems to show itself as critical and essential throughout most stages of the innovation process.

As we wrote in a recent article, "Listening intently and being aware of all the verbal and nonverbal cues in communication is harder than most of us admit. There's a strong psychological phenomenon called *confirmation bias* in which human beings tend to search for, focus on, and see information that confirms beliefs or opinions they already hold, especially if the issue at hand is emotionally charged. Noticing details and listening openly is a key behavior needed to increase our innovation fitness. As we already discussed, innovation is rooted in both discovering needs and insights from the environment as well as collaborating with teammates and stakeholders on finding a solution" (Imaretska and Sweeney 2015).

Think of how many different ways we have to listen in order to innovate. We need to listen to our customers in ways that tell us more than just what we should build for them in order to determine what they *really* need. Sometimes they don't know—so we have to listen for them. We need to listen to ourselves, our instincts, our guts—both to find sparks of innovation and to identify our own innovative barriers or biases. Our fear.

We define the term *listening* pretty broadly. It's about awareness, being present, taking what you think is your ability to hear, see, perceive, and empathize, and then cranking it up 100 times. It's gathering all that is going on around you. It's external and internal—noticing the obvious and picking up on the most subtle things.

Listening is a very selfless act, since one of the first igniters of great listening is to be more curious and investigative of others and of their ideas than of yourself and *your* own ideas. My wife has put it to me this way: "What if we approached each encounter with another person as if there were a strong possibility that *in* that moment that person was about to teach us the most important thing we've ever learned?" When we listen with that much intention and effort it is hard *not* to be in the mindset of discovery.

One of the first self-realizations I had when I began taking improvisation classes was that my understanding of good listening had been adequate or aligned with the norm in the business world. However, it wasn't even *close* to the level of listening I needed to be able to do a good improvisational scene. The revelations were many. The first was that my approach to listening, before I started improvising, was passive. If I was in the same room or in a conversation with others my ears and eyes and brain would pick up on what was going on around me and would gather a large enough amount of information. I was essentially listening by default. I assumed that the way my body was built and the way my brain worked was enough: I had my listening equipment turned on, and that was adequate.

After the first few levels of improvisational training I knew that I needed to listen in a much more intentional and hard-working manner. I began to appreciate the direct relationship between listening and effort. I also realized, as I did with all of the Big Five behaviors, that I could claim accountability for my listening and practice ways to become a better listener. I realized listening wasn't a soft skill; it was an athletic, measurable, improvable innovation asset.

The second revelation was that there is a way to listen with the purpose in mind. The improvisational purpose for listening is to build something. So when I am in the mindset of discovery and performing improvisation, I listen for information as building blocks—things that will help me make my next choice in support of the direction of the scene. I remain open to things that my brain processes as visualizations of the next moment I will create on stage. It's not to collect data, it's to collect building materials and instantly go to work. And it's my favorite type of listening.

The third revelation was that we can *decide* how to listen. We can be intentional and tactical in the way we identify, gather, and process the information that is available to us during listening. I now find myself listening in drastically different ways, depending on the type of information I need, the best way to feed it into my brain, and the way I will ultimately be using it. What I am using the information for is a big factor in the choices I make in my listening tactics. I listen one way in a sales conversation, another way when I am comforting one of our sons, and another way when I am trying to overcome a bias or a preconceived point of view. I am impressed by the level of sophistication and the number of choices that are available in something as simple as listening.

Listening to a City

I became a fan of former Minneapolis mayor R.T. Rybak one night for two different reasons. First, while attending opening night of a show at the Brave New Workshop, he was able to pull off—in great fashion—wearing a pair of khaki cargo pants. Seldom is such a feat seen from the mayor of a major metropolitan city. Second, he didn't seem to mind that we roasted him from the stage in front of 200 people for wearing khaki cargo pants.

To me, politics and innovation seem to be a tricky mix—perhaps because of the whole reelection thing. And yet in my opinion, R.T. seemed more like a chief innovation officer of the city than a typical mayor. He is a designer: always observing, always listening, and always gathering. Our city's diversity increased greatly during his tenure. He responded by listening to more people and by listening differently to make sure he heard what all of the various voices were saying.

Mayor Rybak also is an inspiration to me when it comes to having what is right trump what is popular—again, a tough thing to do in the world of politics. Once the data had been collected and it was clear that he needed to make a decision for the betterment and forward progress of the city, he had his marching orders. He knew when it was time to gather information and points of view and when it was time to put on the blinders to ensure that his focus and energy were properly funneled toward executing the solution.

During his tenure he led efforts in economic development, affordable housing, transportation, and youth violence prevention. When he left office Minneapolis had restored its AAA bond rating, had the lowest unemployment in the country, and had put 20,000 young people through the STEP-UP summer jobs program. Our city is a better city because of his work, and that was also always clear to me as I watched him lead. He is driven by a desire to improve the human condition and serve others. Many times I have seen wonderful human beings enter into the world of politics with great intentions and a true and authentic sense of service—and many times the politics of politics seem to shift their focus and dilute their original motivation. R.T. Rybak didn't let politics distract him from the job of helping others—as is evident from my conversation with him.

John: I know a lot about innovation in the corporate world because it's focused on new products and new ways to reach customers. But as you're growing a city—and improving the lives of a large group of people—how do you define *community innovation*? What does the word innovation mean to someone who has viewed the world from your perspective?

R.T.: I don't think there are huge new strategies; the best way to nurture community innovation is to stop thinking about it and focus more on listening to multiple voices. There are so many different voices involved in cities, so they have a natural innovation process due to having a variety of perspectives. If you are truly listening to a city's many citizens, you can't move in the same direction—because the cities, by nature, are just where people's ideas intersect and collide.

I hate to compare my constituents to coffee grounds and wilted lettuce, but innovation in the city is a lot like compost. You just have to turn it all the time. That's where the energy is.

John: That's awesome. Listening is so essential for innovation to happen. In improvisation, if we have five disparate points of view on stage at the same time—multiple perspectives, as you just said—innovation will happen organically just because we're presenting the intersection of those five points of view.

R.T.: Yeah. If you think about how cities formed, they were places where different people with different interests came together. They are where you get one plus one is three. Many people, many perspectives in one place. You can't help but create something new. Change is a constant in a place where you're listening to lots of different voices.

John: That's a really interesting point of view from a leader—of a city, or a small group. That really says that the innovation will come from the organic conversation if it's monitored well. It's different from a leader saying, "I know what the city ought to do, and this is what we're going to go do." It's really kind of a listening and servant approach to what the next innovation should be.

You see some leaders in politics and in business who approach their job from a perspective of, "I've done my data research, and now I'm going to choose and this is what I think." That's a much different thing from what you're talking about.

R.T.: It is.

After my conversation with the mayor—the first one we had had since he'd been back in the civilian population—I was really impressed with the duality of his behaviors. I'd never realized that his job required him to live in such broad areas of the innovation mindset. At the beginning of a new city initiative he was an amazing example of listening. He listened to so many different points of view—most of which contrasted with each other, and many of which might have contrasted with his own viewpoint.

R.T. employed more than one of the Big Five behaviors to be successful, as we'll hear about later in the book. After he gathered information and analysis had taken place he had to enlist a very strong level of declaration. He had to be persuasive in his communications and unrelenting in support of the direction he was advocating. It was almost as if different parts of the process required different types of innovation behaviors.

Many people are great listeners, but, unlike R.T., can't make declarative decisions. Others are good at not judging things but are sometimes hesitant to move to action. R.T. has learned that innovation behaviors are necessary in different ways for different parts of the innovation process. I was very impressed to learn more about his talent for moving from listener to active leader in such a decisive and seemingly natural style. I can't wait to see what he has in store for his new passion:

transforming education. He's now the executive director of Generation Next, where he's working to make Minneapolis and St. Paul national leaders in innovative, cradle-to-career approaches to youth development.

Listening and Innovation

I love the many roles that listening can play in the innovation culture and process. One of the great results of listening fully to someone you are collaborating with is that she instantly feels validated and respected. This leads to authenticity and trust, which leads to better ideas. It's a circle of awesomeness.

Listening is also a powerful tool for stopping the inner dialogue about what *should* be the outcome or executable, that this is how we've always done it before, or that this is what I'm most comfortable with. It seems as if listening distracts our negative inner voice. We have a finite amount of attention to give—and if we choose to give it all to the person we are listening to, we are no longer giving any attention to the self-judging, negative self-talk that sometimes is playing in our head like bad talk radio.

Another great role listening plays in innovation is that it serves as a vehicle to get you into a pool of ideas beyond your current understanding. When our heads are fighting us the whole way, sometimes traveling to that pool can be quite a battle.

When I intentionally put on my listening hat, especially when listening to people who are much different than I am, I'm very quickly taken into a new realm. I am a stowaway on someone else's idea ship. Their ideas take me to new perspectives, to new angles: It's not just new information that I'm gaining from them, it's the ability to look at the entire question or challenge differently than I ever would have if I had stayed within my own head.

Harken Health's Ryan Armbruster agrees that listening is a critical behavior and that curiosity plays a big role in being able to open up our perspective to embrace opportunity:

Ryan: You've got to be willing to explore. You've got to be willing to ask questions, try things. I think that's so important. If you're not curious, not asking questions or challenging things, or asking why, you're probably not going to put your finger on the next innovation opportunity.

I'm really big on curiosity. Curiosity is something that you can nurture a little bit, but it's also something some people just have. As in anything, some people are more naturally inclined to it than others. I'm looking for that natural talent; oftentimes it's acute.

John: I'm a big believer that you can always go and practice being curious.

Ryan: Definitely. I think a key skill related to that is understanding what's happening—being aware, watching what's going on and picking up on cues.

It's something that we have to tune out over time because there's just so much going on in the world. Not only with respect to information and media; the world is a busy place and just from a sanity point of view you have to tune out a lot of it. But you're actually tuning out what could be a lot of interesting learning, insight, and perspectives, and a lot of things that you could be doing that a lot of people are missing. A lot of people tune it out. We need to ask ourselves, "How do I pay attention to things? How do I see things that maybe aren't really obvious to people?"

A dozen years ago I was working with design researchers who spent all of their time nurturing their skills of observation and curiosity. This was before I was really getting into it. We went to a coffee shop and did an exercise there to give me some skills and tool sets. I was thinking, "Oh, this is so cool. I'm going to be able to do really good things."

I went to that coffee shop and I totally cased the joint. I thought I learned everything that was going on there. I came back, super excited. As the experts gave their point of view I fell off my chair. It wasn't necessarily that I didn't *see* the same things, because I was sitting in the same darn coffee shop that they were. It was what they *chose to see* and how they interpreted the things that they were seeing that I completely wasn't tuned into. It gave me a really deep appreciation for the skill set that you can develop around observation and curiosity.

John: I'm interested in empathy as a way of listening. One of the things I'm most proud of is that when my sons are in a group or there is a kid or a person who's clearly showing signs of need, maybe emotional need, and my boys notice and address that. When my boys go and start playing catch with someone on their Little League team because it's clear from his body language that he's a little sad that day or that he's maybe not a great athlete so no one's playing catch with him, I think, "They noticed, they noticed more than the other kids."

Being empathetic means we have to notice people's behavior, not just the color of their clothes or how they're walking. We really have to read them. That's all within that kind of listening that we talked about.

Ryan: Yeah, you got it. There are so many cues out there and tuning into those cues is critical. I think that we usually tune them out pretty quickly. They're out there and we can use them to be so much more insightful.

Listening and Persuasion

Listening also plays a big role in the process of selling or socializing your ideas and innovations. When you're in a situation that calls for persuasion, you have to be in tune with the person or people you're trying to persuade. I often coach the sales groups I work with on picking up and hearing what is important to their prospects, and then tailoring their presentations, information, or pitches to what they've heard. That may involve being especially present and observant in the moment, or it may mean spending some extra time preparing and doing your homework on the people who can fund or support your idea. Make the conversation about them, speak their language, and connect with them on a human level through listening—and you will be pleased with the results.

I can't tell you how many times I have seen great ideas or great initiatives fall by the wayside, without budgets or executive traction, because the individuals who are championing them don't have the skills to move them through the organizational process. As you pitch or evangelize your innovations, don't forget that you need to incorporate a bit of sales into your innovation advocacy. That's where listening comes in. Great salespeople know that everything they need to close the deal can come from their prospects' mouths if they simply ask the right questions and listen carefully. If you believe that there are individuals or parts of the organization that may shut down your idea or not support your initiative ask them what's important, ask them what type of innovations they're looking for, ask them about innovations they respect and love. Ask them what they think the solution looks like and what aspirations they have when it comes to the problem they are asking you to solve. Do everything you can to get inside their heads and understand how they view the problem and what would be most attractive to them in an innovation that provides the solution to the problem, an innovation that they would support and perhaps fund.

Listen for what they want and then evangelize your idea in a way that gives them what they said they needed. I don't mean drastically change your innovation, I mean position it and communicate it in a way that it gets heard and approved. The only way you'll know how to do that is to listen.

My wife Jenni is one of the co-founders of Gilda's Club Twin Cities. It is a wonderful clubhouse environment that provides social and emotional support for anyone who is on the cancer journey: patients, families, friends, and survivors—anyone. For a while, especially right after the recession, it seemed almost impossible to reach the fundraising goal of $5 million that she needed to open the clubhouse. And yet little by little, always gaining momentum, always reaching the next small milestone, she did it! In 2014 the doors opened and now there is a place in the Twin Cities where people can go and face cancer with the support of a community and programming, completely free of charge.

I watched Jenni and sometimes accompanied her throughout the years as she approached large donors. Oftentimes she would hear from them their opinion about why Gilda's Club wasn't needed in the Twin Cities, or, more consistently, the reasons that they were not able to contribute. The most common phrase she used to handle those objections was, "Tell me more about that." When they shared more, she diligently wrote down everything she heard as if it were her to-do list. Then—sometimes weeks, sometimes months, sometimes years later—she would meet with them again with that same handwritten list and she would let them know that she had heard all of their valid objections and that she wanted to simply let them know what she had done to address—and many times overcome—those objections. They felt heard and honored that she had taken the time to look into the things they were concerned about, and they would get out their checkbooks and generously help her create Gilda's Club Twin Cities.

Her listening was her best fundraising talent!

APPLICATION EXAMPLE: LISTENING

It's important to listen to your customers, to your colleagues, and to yourself. But it's also critical to listen to disparate people and points of view. Gina Valenti, vice president of owner services for Hilton Worldwide and vice president of brand culture and internal communications for the Hampton brand, recommends listening to voices outside of your industry for ways that can help you—and your company—become more innovative:

"One thing that I've learned over the years is the power of being curious, and exploring, and looking all over for where things are working and how to use that as a springboard. In hospitality you're not going to get a lot of great, innovative, cool, new, thought-sparking ideas when you're just looking at yourself or others like you. You get the great ideas by partnering and looking out at the world of where stuff is working, or where things are sticky, or what people are gravitating toward.

"One of my personal favorite things in my job that I've really been empowered to do is surrounding myself with really smart, creative, and sometimes wacky people, such as yourself, such as Marcus Buckingham, learning from all types of companies all around the globe and what they're doing to create engagement and to differentiate their brand.

"Years ago, we were at a meeting at corporate, and we were talking about companies that really have a differentiated service culture, and companies like Southwest Airlines and Zappos showed up on the flip chart. Somebody in the room said, 'Someday I hope that Hampton is a brand that people look to for differentiation.' I thought about that yesterday when I was doing a presentation about Hampton's differentiated culture and I thought, 'You know, that's pretty cool that over the last 10 years we've made such great strides in this area.'

"But it's been very intentional; it hasn't been haphazard. It's been a very intentional journey."

Listening Fitness Plan and Workouts

To enable us to practice listening intentionally and effectively, we've broken down listening into several so-called "muscles" you can exercise in order to become a better listener:

Muscles to Exercise

1. Controlling your attention.
2. Noticing on different levels: body language, tone, information presented.
3. Interpreting information at both an emotional and intellectual level.
4. Cleansing your bias in order to perceive the truth.
5. Recovering when you lose control of your attention.

As we discussed in Chapter 7, habits are closely linked to our environment and circumstance. So the best way to build habits of effective listening is to hone in on one or two tactics you can employ in your daily life immediately and to build triggers for yourself that will remind you to behave as a good listener. Here are five straightforward *tactics* that you can employ in any conversation:

Tactics to Practice

1. Repeat what you heard before you respond.
2. Eliminate distractions.
3. Decide to listen before you begin to listen.
4. Be intentional about your biases and decide to listen openly for a controlled amount of time.
5. Assume there will be value in what you are about to hear and that your job is to uncover it.

Now choose which tactic you would like to employ at least once a day for the next week. Write down the specific actions you

(Continued)

will take to ensure you use the tactic. These could be things such as a reminder on your phone that's set for one minute before a meeting that says "Decide to listen," a Post-it note on your computer screen that says "Uncover the value," a morning reminder to eliminate distractions during the meetings or calls you have that day, putting your phone away when you're talking to someone, and closing your laptop (or not even bringing it) when you are in a meeting.

In addition to triggering the listening behavior in your daily activities, there are ways you can intentionally create *listening workouts*. Below we've highlighted 10 ways you can strengthen your listening "muscles":

1. Watch a movie in a different language to see how much of the plot, emotions, conflict, and humor you can pick up on.
2. Listen to talk radio or sports radio that drastically differs from your own point of view. Make yourself listen for 10 minutes and then try to write down three things you heard that you agree with.
3. Listen to old radio shows with your eyes closed and try to see if you can picture the environment they are describing. Can you be in the same scene with the characters?
4. Find an instructional video on the web. Listen first in a way that allows you to remember as much of the specific information as you can, as if you are going to be tested on the accuracy of the words you heard. Listen a second time and pick up just the important pieces of information you'll need to do whatever the video pertains to (e.g., creating a meal, building a birdhouse, or changing a tire). Then listen a third time, with the goal of being able to teach someone else the same information. Notice that you have listened three different ways.
5. Listen to a child who is upset about something—but not with the goal of providing a solution. The goal is to see if you can demonstrate empathetic listening, which by itself may bring the child what she needs.

6. Listen to a presentation on the web that focuses on a topic or piece of content that you are completely uninterested in. Notice how long it takes for your mind to wander and then do your best to get back into effective and focused listening.

7. Try to come up with a list of new names for products, or song titles, or new political parties. Pause after you write down each new idea or item and see if you can hear any internal commentary on what you just wrote down.

8. Find a partner and listen to something that is very subjective and perhaps controversial—maybe a newscast clip. Each of you should write down the five most important things you heard in the news story and then compare notes.

9. Find two pieces of music that you have never heard before. Play them on your computer in two different web browsers at the same time. See if you listen to one more intently than the other. See if it's possible to listen to both of them at the same time.

10. Listen to an ad for a luxury resort or cruise line, perhaps one that you have considered before. Write down the information that is important to you. Now listen to the same ad as if you were someone without much education or opportunity that lives below the poverty line. Write down your thoughts from that point of view.

9

Deferring Judgment

D eferring judgment is the Big Five behavior that perhaps gets misinterpreted most often. We forget to focus on the word *defer* and somehow replace it with *eliminate* or *avoid*. Sometimes that leads us to the point of view of "I know we're not supposed to be too judgmental, but if you don't judge things how can you figure out what's best?"

To be able to refine, analyze, and make great decisions, you do need to have a healthy dose of judgment. You must evaluate and understand what things *won't* work as you implement innovative ideas. However, all of that necessary judgment should come a bit later in the innovation process. How much later depends on the process itself, although most of our clients are surprised at how just a few minutes of deferring judgment can enrich the thinking and the pool of ideas and possibilities a team gets to work with.

So the active word here is *defer*. This behavior is really about that first move—the question of "What is the first thing I do when something new comes my way?" What I found to be of value—and what I suggest others practice—is to simply put some space between the moment that the new information comes our way and the beginning of the judgment process. *To defer is simply to wait a bit.* During that time and in that space judgment *limits* possibility and potential, while deferring judgment *multiplies* possibility and potential.

As we learned in our chapter on fear, when we are under stress our automatic responses of fight, flight, or freeze kick in. They block our executive functions, which allow us to experience empathy and carry out more complex thought processes. Moreover, we are constantly scanning our environment for threats and rewards and subconsciously classifying every piece of information and every moment through that lens. Because we know that's our tendency, it's important to incorporate deferring judgment as part of our innovation fitness workout. This will help us to be inclusive in our thinking and to not eliminate anything just because we automatically classified it as a threat or reacted from a place of fear.

A great place to start when it comes to practicing the behavior of deferring judgment is to assume that the new information or circumstance entering your life is neutral—that it's just information, a generic circumstance that for at least a moment is neither good nor bad. In trying to do this more often, I have noticed that when I consciously choose a neutral reaction to something new, many times it at least gives me a fifty-fifty chance of finding something good or positive in that moment. Every day there is something new that comes into my life, and I realize in hindsight that if I had judged it immediately it would've been a completely uninformed, reactive, and perhaps irrational judgment. With innovation, it's dangerous—and certainly inefficient and ineffective—to have judgment be your go-to, default response. One example: In the fall of 2014 I received an e-mail from the new owner of our old building, which came as a surprise to me as I didn't even know that the building had been sold. This meant that we had to relocate our school from a facility we had occupied for 48 years in just 75 days. I somehow was able to find a way to react neutrally. And that initial reaction of neutrality allowed me to jump-start and expedite finding a solution instead of being angry or worried.

Deferring judgment also has a mathematical benefit. If we can create a space between stimulus and judgment, we can fill that space with new information, our teammates' points of view, a new version of the same information, and countless other manifestations that simply would've been unavailable or blocked if we had immediately judged. The simple analogy that always comes to mind when discussing this topic is from my upbringing on the farm. I can hear my father's voice saying to me as a young boy, "Remember, a covered seed will never grow."

That's how it feels to me when an idea or a new circumstance encounters judgment right away: Any and all growing potential, in whatever form that might take, has been shut down.

Sometimes it makes sense to defer judgment for a split second or two. However, other times—especially if you've been putting out fires fast and furiously for a while—it may make sense to do something more drastic and put a larger amount of space between stimulus and judgment. For my good friend Jacquie Berglund, it means putting everything on pause and heading off into the woods to hit the reset button and reconnect with what's important. Jacquie is the co-founder and CEO of FINNEGANS, Inc., a social enterprise that donates 100 percent of its profits from the sale of its beer to alleviate hunger in the Midwest. With a small team and limited resources—and absolutely achievable aspirations to change the world—Jacquie often finds herself feeling the pressure to keep the momentum going.

John: As much as I work on deferring judgment, there are days when something comes my way and my reaction is, "Oh, no!" or "Why me?" or "This is anything but awesome." What do you do when you start to flail like that?

Jacquie: I remember one time when I was just living in fear and restriction and freaking everyone else out on my team; nobody wins on that deal. So I had to do a bunch of mental therapy—which for me means going out to my house in the woods and just getting away from everything and calming myself down and getting quiet. It's an opportunity for a lot of self-talk as well as conversations with my sister, who provides me with great support.

John: It seems as if doing this also helps you to redefine or reconnect with that inner voice, that greater good, that life of value. It tells me that if we clearly define the "why we do this," when times get tough or we doubt ourselves we can reconnect to that "why." Then that will help us reframe and get back to the place of discovery. If we're not in the place of discovery and confidence, we'll never get to where we need to be.

Jacquie: Yeah, you can't move; it's paralyzing. The trick is determining our own processes for how to do that. We're busy people who often don't realize when we're going a million miles an hour. I have to take everything that is my person, my essence, and my spirit and calm it down and slow it down. You have to be very purposeful about "I will go and spend two days in the woods now. I'm so busy, I'm so stressed, I think this is the stupidest thing for me to not be working for a couple of days, but I must."

Convincing yourself that getting away is a logical good move is very hard when everything's falling apart. That, to me, seems against human nature. But we have to identify these systems, make conscious choices about our processes, and then be very, very thoughtful and present to move to a discovery space.

John: There's nothing like being in that place of fear and worry, and then you get in the car and you head toward the woods. And then on the way back you're kind of different; you experienced this transformation so there's obviously a change of pace and that helps your body. There's a lack of distractions.

Jacquie: Yeah, I shut everything out. Nature's very healing for me—especially water. I have a small lake, so if I'm even looking at the water—or swimming around, or in the boat, or whatever I'm doing—it's very calming.

John: Is it that you feel less hectic and then new ideas are clear, or is it that you're also reconnecting to that inner voice?

Jacquie: It's reconnecting, for sure. Meditation doesn't work for me, because I can't sit long. I walk or I go take bubble baths instead. Everyone has to find what works for them.

John: I think even as scattered as people like us are, you get quiet, you get uncluttered and that reconnecting happens because of what you're doing and you've made that conscious choice to go out in the woods again.

We'll hear more from Jacquie later in the book.

Deferring Judgment to Aid Collaboration

Innovation works best when many diverse points of view have a chance to mingle and cocreate. A team of researchers recently showed that organizations with diverse employees and leaders with inclusive behaviors are 70 percent more likely to capture a new market and 45 percent more likely to expand an existing one (Hewlett, Marshall, Sherbin, and Gonsalves 2013). For the magic of diversity to work, employees have to practice deferring judgment about different and perhaps opposing points of view so that they can collaborate effectively.

Innovation is a collaborative process. It's therefore vital that we have others react to, improve upon, add to, and affect our ideas. In improvisation, we call it the *declaration* and the *reaction*, which are the building blocks of what we are creating. This two-step process occurs in every new moment of an improv scene. Since each moment is based upon—and relies upon—the previous one, it's clear that the strength of the foundation and beginning of the scene is directly related to the success and quality of the rest of the scene.

Great innovation dynamic seems to usually have an exponential quality; it's explosive, it's fast, and it's exciting. That energy and pace that we all have experienced when teams are innovating well comes from and is fueled by the lack of judgment in the first part of the process. This sets the stage for team trust and going places we would not have been able to go on our own.

When we are in the right mindset, the space we create by deferring judgment is most often filled with a forward-moving and often positive addition, or improving upon the idea or moment that was just introduced. *When we defer judgment, we create the space that's needed to allow the next part of innovation to happen.* It's much like a series of dominoes: The space between the dominoes is as important as the dominoes themselves.

Avoiding Judgment Plaque

As a professional speaker, I'm asked almost daily to defer judgment about the audience I am speaking to. When I first began to speak I found myself creating biases almost immediately after the speech was booked. I would find myself thinking things such as, "Awesome, 350 actuaries. This is going to be a party!" Or, "An after-dinner speech with mobile-phone salespeople, 85 percent male, after a golf outing and an open bar. I'm sure they'll be both attentive and respectful!" But I've found over the years, time and time again, that my biases were ridiculously off base. And many times any preconceived judgment I might've had about an audience ended up being further from reality than I could've imagined.

So eventually, and to the benefit of my speeches and my career, I now just assume that every audience I speak to will be awesome. And for the most part they are. This longer-tail level of deferring judgment is different from deferring judgment in a brainstorming session and shows me another benefit. I typically book my speeches six months in advance—so judging an audience prematurely gives me six months of potentially built-up judgment. That *judgment plaque* has a tendency to build up and grow over any given period of time. I could've used all of those moments I spent judging in other ways, such as preparing for the speech, learning more about the audience, and exploring new and innovative ways to help them and add value to the event. And although I still agree that a certain level of judgment is needed in any development process, the previous example about my keynote audiences also demonstrates that it's hard to simultaneously innovate and improve while in a mindset of fear and judgment.

APPLICATION EXAMPLE: DEFERRING JUDGMENT

One simple area in which I'm trying to practice and get better at deferring judgment is in my life as a professional e-mailer. I think if many of us chose honest job titles that reflected what we do most often, all of us would have business cards and e-mail signatures that declare to the world, "I am a professional e-mailer." It's therefore incredibly important to apply this practice to this particular area of our work lives.

I practice deferring judgment in my in-box. I often feel as if I have to act immediately when I hear that wonderful Microsoft chime that so kindly alerts me to a new e-mail. My feeling of urgency is drastically increased if I think that the e-mail deserves a swift and mighty dose of judgment. You know the feeling—when an e-mail chain feels more like a boxing match? So, I have tried to get in the practice of simply waiting—sometimes hours, sometimes days. I have found that the reply I send after putting some space in between my reaction and my action is much different than the one I would've sent impulsively when in the mindset of judgment.

When I defer judgment and put space in between receiving the e-mail and responding to it I am able to look at the e-mail differently, scale back my emotional response, and see the sender's point of view in a much more empathetic way. Oftentimes I'm also filled with new ideas that get us closer to the solution and out of the e-mail Pugil Stick fight!

Deferring Judgment Fitness Plan and Workouts

As with the listening behavior we covered in Chapter 8, to enable us to practice deferring judgment effectively we've broken down the behavior into several "muscles" you can exercise in order to become a more patient information receiver:

Muscles to Exercise:

1. Pausing.
2. Employing gratitude.
3. Embracing "what if" versus "it's not going to work because."
4. Letting go of preconceived notions and biases.
5. Calming your emotions to let the cortical brain do its work.

Tactics to Practice:

1. Take a timed pause before responding. Depending on the circumstances, you can decide to wait a few moments, a few hours, or even a few days.
2. Say thank you—and really mean it—before responding.
3. Say "yes, and" as a conjunction.
4. Survey your body and relax it intentionally. Breathe.
5. Put yourself in other people's shoes to find value in their points of view.

Once again choose which tactic you would like to employ at least once a day for the next week. Write down the specific actions you will take to ensure you use the tactic. This could be things such as a reminder on your phone that's set for one minute before a meeting that says "Pause before you respond," a Post-it note on your computer screen that says "Breathe," literally beginning your sentences with "Yes, and," and creating a prewritten paragraph to use as the need arises that says you will respond after you have had a chance to consider the matter.

In addition to triggering the deferring judgment behavior in your daily activities, there are ways you can intentionally create

(Continued)

deferring judgment workouts. We've highlighted five ways you can strengthen your deferring judgment "muscles":

1. Stage family debates on fun or silly topics such as the merits of playing sports in high school, styling dogs into cubes (that's a thing, apparently!), or choosing Patagonia for your vacation spot. Argue for one side and then switch sides and repeat the exercise.
2. Take the implicit bias test from Harvard Business School (https://implicit.harvard.edu/implicit/takeatest.html) and surround yourself with images that address the biases you uncover.
3. Practice breathing exercises and meditation to help you slow down and calm your emotions when you need to.
4. Find five ideas that were considered crazy at the time they were first introduced but are now accepted as being true (such as thinking the world is round). Reflect upon the value of deferring judgment on those ideas, which helped them become accepted.
5. Write down a current challenge you are working on and think through how various people you know—colleagues, relatives, even friends—would perceive it and solve it.

10

Declaring

Xiong
Wow, what a meeting!

Jasmine
I know. You could cut the tension with a knife.

Xiong
Right? When she opened the meeting with "I really want to know how you feel," I knew we were in for something epic!

Jasmine
When she was like, "Tell me what it's like to work here," I was like, most days, it's great; but there are a few things that really wear on me and make it difficult for me to get excited to work here some days.

Xiong
I know. And when she brought up the new office configuration, I was like, all we would have to do is move a few pieces of furniture, and this would be so much more collaborative.

Jasmine
Yep. And when she talked about needing our opinions on the new strategy and direction I was like, if I actually knew or understood the strategy and direction, I would have an opinion.

Xiong
Me, too. Then she asked for ideas about ways we can improve. There were all those things that you and I talked about last week.

Jasmine
I know. I had a bunch of new ones, too.

Xiong
I was *so close* to saying something.

Jasmine
Me, too. There were like three times when I almost raised my hand and said something.

Xiong
Maybe next time.

Jasmine
Yeah. Where should we go for lunch?

I 've always described the feeling of being in a great improv scene as akin to a form of surfing—on a flying magic carpet. The speed is exhilarating, the direction is unpredictable, there are ups and downs, and yet there is no fear. No fear of falling, of misdirection, of what's next. That lack of fear is based on two conditions: One, the improvisers are in the mindset of discovery, and two, strong declarations have been made at the beginning of the scene.

For an improviser, a declaration signals the *start*, but perhaps more importantly builds the *foundation* of the scene that is about to occur. The strength of that foundation (the carpet that you are riding upon) relies on the quality of the initial declarations the improvisers have made. A declaration means letting each other, our teammates, and the audience know who we are, where we are, what our point of view is, and what we want to accomplish in the scene.

A strong declaration is one that is clear, concise, authentic, and rich in content.

There's a very real relationship between the strength of the declarations and the level of safety the participants in the scene feel. The same holds true for any conversation, brainstorming session, or innovation process. The declarations that we make—and the clarity with which we communicate our ideas, our points of view, and the information that we are trying to share—all can make us and others who may have feelings somewhere on the spectrum between confused and not confident, move to safe and engaged.

Declarations are vital to the innovation process—because much like an improvisational scene, most innovation processes, whether big or small, short-lived or long-term, seem to have some level of iteration. And because of that iteration, the *next* moment is always somehow affected and reliant on the *last* moment. This domino effect always seems to go better if it is given a great start. That's why strengthening our declaration muscles is so important for innovation.

Another reason declaring plays an important role is because it can reduce fear and increase engagement among the members of the team driving the innovation process. I have watched countless groups of excited and willing team members go from "This is going to be great!" to "I'm not sure what to do next" to "I lost my passion for this initiative"—simply because vague and general declarations were made at the beginning. You want to introduce clear and declarative information from the very start to set up your team for success.

My speaking career has always depended on creating safety and engagement through strong declarations. I began giving public presentations on innovation in 2001. Every time, whether it's in my introduction or in the first few moments of my speech, the audience members become fully aware that they are about to participate in activities associated with the word *improvisation*—and many times they won't have known this before the speech.

When I break the news to them it usually sounds like, "In the next 90 minutes we are going to dive headfirst into the world of improvisational theater." Whether it's an audience of 50 or 5,000, there is always a reaction—sometimes even an audible one. There is a healthy amount of eye rolling, uncomfortable shifting in seats—and occasionally, in some people's eyes, sheer terror. And there I am: 60 seconds into my speech, a collaborative experience whose goal is to help strangers begin their journey from fear to discovery. And most of them are either scared to death or relatively angry at me. It's awesome!

So I declare—strongly, authentically, and with as much clarity as I possibly can. The purpose and goal of my declaration is to provide the members of my audience with my point of view and enough information about the next moments of their lives to make them feel safe enough to participate and be engaged. My definition of engaged means they will get out of their seats, walk up on stage, and participate in an improvisational innovation exercise in front of a crowd. That level of engagement takes a level of safety and encouragement that's a little bit higher than filling out an online survey.

So *what* do I declare to try to accomplish those goals? I let them know that I am *grateful* to be with them and to be getting paid for what I'm doing. I let them know that my role is to *serve* them, not to tell them things. And I let them know that the *energy* that I will produce while we're together will be big, loud, unpredictable, and somewhat irreverent.

I also clarify what's going to happen. I let them know that I'm not going to try to ask them to be funny, or even teach them how to be a comedic improviser. I explain that our time together will be structured within the liberal arts learning model—that we will simply use improvisation as a metaphor and as a way to look at our own innovative behaviors through a different lens.

During my presentation I impart information about what will happen. I describe the exercises I will ask them to do in a way that is both accurate and disarming. I often describe the exercises as "Outward Bound for the mind" and let them know that people just like them do these exercises every single day.

There's also a bit of challenge in my declaration. I let them know that I haven't found a way to get better at things or to improve my innovative abilities without some level of awkwardness and discomfort. I reinforce that there can be no improvement without practice and that practice isn't always easy. I introduce them to our learning model as a way to show where we are headed, and I say that I believe that all of us can practice behaviors that allow us to spend more time in the mindset of discovery.

I ask for their permission and trust. And once I have it, we begin.

Declaring for Innovation

Now let's talk about the math of innovation. As we mentioned before, the level of diversity in points of view is a clear indicator of how rich an innovation can be. But the conduit or vehicle to get those points of view into the equation is clearly *how well they are communicated. That's* the declaration! I know there are times when politics, emotions, or processes give us excuses to avoid stating our points of view. But if we take the subjectivity out of such a statement and look at it simply as a math equation it becomes a bit less messy. If our job is to participate in innovation (which, by the way, I believe is *everybody's* job), then the only way we can actually do that is to add our points of view—to include our individual diversity variable into the equation.

Declaring is a simple act of adding what we have to the innovation equation. This framework of the innovation process is probably why I don't have much tolerance for people who don't declare their points of view. If you find yourself hesitating, study the reasons why. Could it be a communication channel issue? Give yourself permission to declare in a way that works best for you. If you are not an extrovert loudmouth like me, it is perfectly okay to submit your point of view in other ways, such as e-mails or handwritten letters or drawings or sketches. Whatever works best—it is our responsibility, all of us, to find a way to declare our points of view. The rest of the team and the people that the solution will serve are counting on us.

It's imperative to find the best way for us to declare our points of view, no matter what the environment or process throws our way. And our environment—whether it's our workplace, customers, or coworkers—can often put up a considerable number of hurdles. Former Minneapolis mayor R.T. Rybak and I talked about ways to continue to innovate when everything and everyone seems to be saying no:

John: I'm wondering about the endurance it must take to continue to strive for positive innovation and believe in positive innovation when the system sometimes doesn't support it. In politics, you have to vote on things. You only have a certain budget. There are a lot of nos in politics—lots of things that can't get done. I always think that's probably why I wouldn't be able to do it: Because I would get beaten down, or tired, or cynical about that inability to execute. Tell us about how a person can continue to accept that that might be the system, whether it's politics or business. What motivates you? How are you able to continue to go forward when a lot of the stuff you want to happen doesn't get done right away?

R.T.:   I honestly don't think it's that much harder to innovate in government and politics than it is in the private sector. I've been in the public sector, the private sector, and the civic sector. Government is frankly *not* all that different as far as innovation goes.

The biggest problem is that political leaders self-edit and try to come up with solutions that they think everybody wants—and you can't do that. The one way I was able to really make a difference was when I stopped trying to be liked so much and spent more time worrying about being respected. The best decisions I made were often ones that, at the time, the majority of people around me didn't agree with. The term is *leader*, not *pollster*.

If you're going to try to move people somewhere, part of what you're paid for is what you bring to the table. You have to listen a lot to people, but if all you were supposed to do is figure out what the majority of people would do, you could put a pet goat in office and give it a yes or no on the poll. Politics gets complicated and difficult when people try to please everybody or reinvent who they are. Right now the most diabolical political weapon is authenticity. Just be yourself and try to synthesize a lot of voices—but at the end of the day listen to your own.

John: One of the things that people can develop when they're working on their innovation behaviors is that kind of resilience or focus you need when others are opposed to your idea. That happens a lot in the middle management layer. Someone really believes in an innovation but then Legal says no. Finance says no. HR says no. That person needs to continue championing the idea, as you just described, right?

R.T.: Right.

John: When you were in those places—perhaps surrounded by people who were disagreeing with you—what kept driving you forward? Was it because you knew that the idea would help people?

R.T.: I had a lot of trouble early on because I couldn't quite figure out how to keep people happy if I needed to do something unpopular. I had the strange gift of walking into a massive financial crisis, under which it was literally impossible to please everyone. In fact, I angered most of the people who supported me in the first six months.

That provided a certain liberation that allowed me to say, "You know, I'm not going to make everyone happy no matter what I do. I have to hear what they say, but at the end of the day I have to make a tough choice here." Then, miraculously, a lot of people who didn't support that idea wound up respecting how I got there. There were those who didn't, who decided that they would never support me because they disagreed on one single issue. But I probably wouldn't have been able to please them for much longer anyway.

Grounding Your Declarations

We've talked a lot about declaring your point of view, sharing your opinions and ideas to build innovation and drive change. You might be wondering, though—what if I don't have anything to declare? What if I am not sure how to move forward or what to contribute?

First of all, we don't necessarily advocate that you make up your mind prior to every meeting, interaction, or ideation session. Sometimes a declaration as simple as "I am open to listening and being affected by others' insights before I add any ideas or opinions" is a very valid one. The art of declaring requires being truthful, authentic, and clear and thus letting those around you know where you stand, so that you as a group can move forward in the most productive manner.

Second of all, knowing where you stand in the grand scheme of things can help you articulate your declarations and ground them in your values. Becoming clear on your mission in life and what you hope to accomplish can be a very helpful tool to bring consistency and clarity to your efforts.

Mission Accomplished

We talked a little with Jacquie Berglund earlier, as she told her story of heading off to the woods to reconnect with what's important. If you knew her, you'd understand even more how amazing it is that she's able to settle down enough to get quiet. Many people tell me that it is not necessarily possible that there is enough energy in any single room for Jacquie and me to be in it together. She is a nonstop, on-fire, smile-ear-to-ear advocate and evangelist for the wonderful mission that she started—and the organization that gets it done.

Every night there are people in Minnesota enjoying a pint of FINNEGANS beer, and every night there are people in Minnesota who don't have enough to eat. Jacquie figured out a way to connect those two.

Her journey is anything but typical; it's one filled with international education, U.N.-level diplomacy, unlikely connections, and an irrepressible personality of positivity. She is relentless in her drive to spend each moment of each day improving the human condition. And the level of innovation she has created to accomplish that daily and life goal is beyond belief.

Jacquie is a great example of how necessary it is to combine ideas, process, structure, and people. Her ideas flow like her beer out of a giant brain vat. Her organization's social entrepreneurship structure and the process by which she connects people in the fight to alleviate hunger are astounding. Without huge budgets—and with a staff of only three or fewer on any given day—she has raised hundreds of thousands of dollars and helped thousands of people. Her army of volunteers is one of the keys to her success. She is a walking case study for the power of an organized group of engaged humans.

But perhaps most importantly, like many great entrepreneurs who are service driven, she is now taking her ideas and multiplying them for others. In 2014 Jacquie received a Bush Fellowship to create a social innovation lab to help other social entrepreneurs get started. Many would've stopped at simply being the founder and caretaker of the only beer-driven social entrepreneurship venture that gives all of its profits away. Not Jacquie: She is driven to create systems, process, and plans that will enable passionate innovators to benefit from her experience and her model. She spoke to me about what drives her:

Jacquie: Some people have a really hard time identifying and understanding their passions, because mission comes from passion. I think about how we identify how we've been living our lives and our focus on service. It's passions within us; those are inside.

I think a lot of people live never knowing their passions; it's really hard to create a mission if you don't know your passions. The first step is knowing yourself—the things that you do that don't seem like work. To me, a passion is something you could do all day long without it feeling like work. It's fun. It brings you joy. That's following your passion.

John: So how do you connect passion and mission?

Jacquie: Building your life around, "How do I utilize my passions to achieve my mission?"—I know a lot of people who miss that part.

It's as if they have no idea what their passions are or how to be true to them. They're the ones who probably aren't going to be meeting their potential.

John: Passion works as a wellspring that also has a north star. It's driving us to do what we think we were built to do. It's the most hopeful thing about the next generation coming into the workplace; they have passion first.

Jacquie: Yeah, I get that. I think we're evolving as human beings. They're way further along than we were.

John: You refer to that passion as your itch—your voice. I think that it's the calling of service.

Jacquie: It's the meaning piece. For 15 years I've had great meaning in my work. I've never lasted at a job more than 5 years, so this is huge for me.

John: What I'm trying to preach is, if you get into a place of service, the need of that human being, those hungry people, and all those people that you fed in the past few years, it will pull you toward service and you won't be worried about "I don't have enough. I don't know enough. I'm not good at this. What if it fails?"

You call it your itch and your voice but there were days when you may have wanted to quit, days you didn't know if it would work. But the bottom line is there are still people without food in this country. When you think about serving through the whole thing you built, is it because you still wake up and say, "We need to feed these people"?

Jacquie: It's something about being here to serve the greater good. How do I transform what is happening in the world so I can be that candle in the darkness? How can I maximize my potential and my skills to fill a need that fits what I'm trying to do? Because in everything you do as a social entrepreneur, from my perspective, you need to be more efficient and effective than the level that already exists.

I'm about working smart. I'm innovative. How can we create something that nobody's done before? You're just going to create huge value for these hungry people, for these local farmers, that is a sustainable model. Everything I do, I think about how I'm going to fund it first.

I think that's why we're here: to maximize our potential. You're given all these gifts and I think so many people died with the music in their hearts. I don't want to be one of those. I'm doing everything I can to maximize what I can put out there.

Jacquie also reminded me that most great innovators are much more concerned with accomplishing their goals than the specific path or series of events that need to happen for them to get them done. Jacquie's path is a great example; she told me that as long as what she created would be of productive and impactful service to the community, she didn't care if the vehicle was a beer company or a lemonade stand. The *how* wasn't nearly as important as the *why*—and like the great innovator she is, she took what she had in her present situation, maximized it, and moved forward. Her declaration and life intent sent her on her way and the beer company was simply a means to fulfilling that declaration.

Communication Is a Two-Way Street

One of the big *aha* moments participants in our training sessions have is that communication is a two-way-street—and that the sender is just as accountable for that information landing appropriately as the receiver is. It can be tempting to use our declarations as a way to send information and be done, to check that one off our list. But *how* you send the information—and ensure it was understood—is part of declaring strongly.

If you are a leader of a team and you continually send e-mails on weekends or late at night, you might be sending more information than you think. In addition to whatever is in the body of your e-mails, you might also be sending the message that your teammates are to reply to you and that you expect them to be working all the time. You might not intend to send this message, but if you have not clarified it previously, you may unwillingly be causing stress or confusion for your team.

If you are on the receiving end of confusing communication, one way to handle it is to declare that you need clarification. In the above example, teammates would benefit most if they clarify the expectations of their leader with respect to the desired timeliness of their responses to e-mails that arrive outside regular working hours, and in this way decrease the stress or uncertainty they might otherwise feel. This might sound like Communications 101, but you would be surprised at how often making assumptions and failing to clarify can put us in a mindset of fear.

Timing your declarations and sending them intentionally can really make a difference in how successful your communication ultimately is. If you are pitching an idea, pursuing funding for your innovation, or trying to influence someone, think through when she would be most focused and receptive and send your declaration at that time. Also, think about her preferred style of communication and what might be most appropriate for your declarations—then create a situation that will set you up for success. If it's an important enough idea, give yourself permission to send a precommunication e-mail or notice to ask the receiver when, where, and how works best for him to give you the focus and attention you and your idea deserve. That might be different depending on the receiver. Some like executive summaries that are clear and short. Some like informal coffee meetings. And some like thorough and data-heavy presentations with the research behind the recommendations. If you can't get that information directly from the person you're communicating with, ask for help from his teammates.

When we took over the theater, we were very intentional in how we held auditions. The industry standard is a relatively high-stress situation, which does not allow applicants to be their best selves. We don't see standing alone on stage in front of a judging panel as the most productive way to get to know a potential employee. We declared that creating a safe place for all our employees, where they can be their most innovative selves, is important to our culture—and that declaration informed the way we structured the audition process. We let applicants know that we want them to succeed and that we can't wait to get to know them. We let the whole applicant group warm up together, we introduce our team, and only then do we begin auditions. At the end of the process, and because we believe in a strong feedback loop, we have a conversation with the applicants about the experience. We offer some honest but kind observations that we hope will help them in their careers and auditions in the future.

We make sure that not only do we create a space for our potential employees to make their declarations successfully, but that we also manifest our organization's declarations in the way we treat human beings and in the way we design processes.

Declaring Nonverbally

I spend the majority of my life either on stage or in front of groups of executives. I am constantly being watched, so I am always aware of what it is that people are watching. As a comedian, I've also realized that I can communicate just as well nonverbally as I can verbally. I would say that in any given performance I get an equal amount of laughs using my body and facial expressions as I do my words. So I am perhaps more aware of the importance of body language than most. That said, I'm still surprised about how little people recognize the significance of their facial expressions, hand gestures, breathing patterns, and overall body language when it comes to declaring.

It shows itself in people using words that proclaim how excited they are—while their bodies are completely still and unengaged. They use words telling people how much they love collaborating or being part of a group—while completely stone-faced and almost menacing. It's an exercise that most people avoid like the plague, but now, especially with mobile phones having such great video capabilities, I can't encourage enough the practice of videotaping yourself as you are conversationally talking about your ideas or points of view. Watching yourself on video is often uncomfortable, so simply take out the emotion and try to identify things you are or are not doing with your body that is sending messages. If we look at our body language as a full distribution channel of information to our audience then we will give it the attention it deserves and intentionally work on using our body language as another asset to declare a point of view.

The Power of Words

Word choice and tone play a bigger part in innovation discussions than we tend to acknowledge. Choosing the right words and approaching the conversation with the right tone is such a vital part of the creative process at the Brave New Workshop. As we are brainstorming, improvising, writing, rehearsing, editing, refining, and performing our scripted shows—which take a group of six to eight people three months to write and get ready for opening night—we are very intentional about how we talk to each other. In general, we do our best to try to separate the work from the person. Not as an effort to dehumanize the work, but as a way to focus our words and tone on the objective and unemotional observation of the work. This eliminates the risk of commenting about the work and having it being attached to the person.

If I say that I don't think your sketch is funny, you may think that I don't think *you* are funny. But if I tell you that I think it would be beneficial for the audience to get to know the characters a bit more at the beginning of the sketch, and that I believe increasing the speed with which the action takes place in the latter part of the scene would build excitement and lead to a great ending of the sketch, you know that I focused on the work and not on you. You also now have some usable action steps instead of a set of words that might simply make you reconsider your theater company career. The same is true in a more traditional workplace. If we can make observations instead of critiques, if we can identify objective improvements to the work without attaching them to the creator of the work, we can reduce workplace drama and optimize the process of cooperation and productivity.

Words play an immense role in corporate culture. One of the things Gina Valenti has taught me is that culture is so much more than a definition and an initiative. Culture is people, and people connecting with other people and treating each other well and doing very human things. I've watched her build that culture in so many different ways, including utilizing the power of words.

John: Tell me about why and how you learned that words really are important.

Gina: This week I was in Omaha at the Gallup organization's annual workplace summit. This is about 200, 250 leaders from probably 50, 60 industries all over the world. This year's focus was organizational identity—purpose, brand, culture. They asked me to come speak to the group about what you were just talking about: What is culture and how does it manifest itself at Hampton?

One of the tips that I shared for how to unleash a culture movement within an organization is to really understand the importance of, how you put it here, words. I always say, "Language matters." I believe that language matters because it aligns people, it rallies people. You have to have a common language in order to create something together. You can't have two people communicating if one is speaking Chinese and the other is speaking English. I've tried that before, with a cab driver in China. We didn't get anywhere. He pulled over onto the side of the road because we weren't understanding each other.

That's really what our culture movement has been centered on at Hampton: creating a common language. We are so intentional about the choice of words that we use and the tone in which we use those words. *Hamptonality* is the word that we use to describe our culture, but it doesn't have a definition, because what brings Hamptonality to life is the unique personality of each of the 60,000 team members worldwide.

Hamptonality is a spin on the word *personality*. All those personalities summed up is Hamptonality, but what it looks like and feels like is going to look and feel as different as the personalities.

If you look at the definition of the word *culture*, it's about how we do things. It's how things feel. Hamptonality has a core set of beliefs, practices, and behaviors, and that's why our values are so important at Hampton.

We have four values: Friendly, Authentic, Caring, and Thoughtful. Those four words, four little words, add a huge impact, because it's a F.A.C.T., get it? Friendly. Authentic. Caring. Thoughtful. It aligns every team member around what Hamptonality should look like, feel like, sound like. It should look and feel friendly, authentic, caring, and thoughtful.

John: The same thing with what you call *moment makers*.

Gina: Right. Moment makers are five ways to make a connection with a guest. When we got rid of scripts in our hotels, we didn't just say, "You don't need a script; just, you know, greet the guest however you want to greet them!" No! We said, "It's really important to make a connection, but make a connection in your authentic way. *Your authentic way.* You might need some tools that help remind you to make a connection, and our moment makers are like a tool belt. They're five ways to connect with guests—whether it's anticipating the guest's need, delivering an unexpected delight, using humor, using empathy, or giving a compliment—in an authentic way.

Some might say, "I'm not so good with humor, but I'm really good at delivering an unexpected delight." So language matters, and it's something that my team and I talk about over and over again.

John: Language matters, especially a word like *Hamptonality*. You can't find that word in the dictionary, but it is part of your language. What I also love about it is that it is a connector by itself; it creates a shared experience for your team members.

Gina: When we first got together with our partners that are developing our Hamptons by Hilton in China, we asked, "What is your take-away and what is your hope for Hampton in China?" One of the leaders from the China group said that Hamptonality is a word spoken and understood by 4 billion people in China!

We like to have fun at Hampton. Hamptonality is just a fun word, but you have to do things with it. The first thing that we did with it is we took the song "You've Got Personality," bought the rights, rewrote it, played with it, and shot the *We've Got Hamptonality* music video.

What we found was, it was sticky, and people started talking about it. That was eight years ago. If you go out to YouTube today you can see our original music video. The word and the idea have been so sticky that now hotels around the world have created their own *We've Got Hamptonality* videos. In Poland, in Russia, in the United Kingdom, they have taken the word and made videos that are very authentic to them.

It's just like any word, right? Words in any language can either become the hottest word used or they can die when they're not used. From a brand-culture perspective you have to support the words that are meaningful to you. I have an internal communications team who is responsible for re-messaging that word and demonstrating it. We do fun things with it, we talk about it, and we sing about it, we dance about it.

We really create an ecosystem of learning and inspiration and professional development that sustains and builds and grows and really unleashes the culture. It's ongoing. We're never done! We just keep going! So we create this ecosystem that feeds the culture, really.

APPLICATION EXAMPLE: DECLARING

Declaring can be an individual behavior, but it can also be something that a group of people engages in together, in one voice. During my discussion with Wanda Howard Battle of the Dexter Avenue King Memorial Baptist Church in Montgomery, Alabama, she told me that her sister Barbara had been a reporter, typist, and associate editor for the *Southern Courier* newspaper. Staffed primarily with college-age students, the *Southern Courier* was published weekly from 1965 to 1968, during one of the most turbulent times in our nation's history. When many national media outlets shied away from covering what was going on in the Deep South, the *Southern Courier* courageously told the world.

John: That must have been very important, because I assume then that the news made its way back to the East Coast, so the paper was telling the truth of what was going on at that point?

Wanda: Absolutely. That's why the students came: To do one-on-one reporting about what was happening in these communities, about civil rights. They were getting a close-up view of it, not just word that was being passed on about what might have been happening. They were a part of it.

John: That was the one thing someone asked the other day: "What did you learn about civil rights on your trip, and specifically, what did you learn about Dr. King?" And I said, I knew he was a preacher and I knew that he was a good orator. But I didn't know how important public relations was. And what a genius he was about making sure that he used the press to really expose the truth. It rang true to me because I don't think the North really knew what was going on down there until Dr. King was able to bring in the TV cameras and the newspapers, such as the one you mentioned—and by doing so, really spread the truth. In some ways, the PR aspect was as important as the politics or the people behind the movement.

Wanda: That is absolutely correct. Once people started seeing the stories, it took the civil rights movement global. People around the world were able to see what was going on and they started to come help in the fight for human rights.

Declarations can take on many forms, from the silly start of an improv scene to the honest point of view shared with your innovation teammates to changing the perception of an entire society. What is important is that we find a way to declare. Practice will help us find the courage to make sure our voices are heard.

Declaring Fitness Plan and Workouts

By now you know the drill. We have broken down *declaring* into several "muscles" you can exercise and have distilled a few tactics you can employ immediately in your everyday interactions to increase the frequency and effectiveness of your declarations.

Muscles to Exercise

1. Speaking up.
2. Verbalizing your emotion.
3. Communicating your observations.
4. Articulating your values and life mission.
5. Closing the feedback loop.

Tactics to Practice

1. Summarize your point of view prior to meetings or encounters, so that you can more easily declare once you are on the spot.
2. Refrain from qualifying statements such as "just spit-balling," "off the top of my head," and "this is probably a terrible idea." Phrases like these instantly devalue your idea and put you in a subordinate relationship with the person you're sharing your idea with.
3. Become aware of your nonverbal declarations and align them with your goals. Literally perform a quick check of your body posture, facial expression, and current activity (e.g., are you looking at your phone?) during encounters to ensure you are projecting the desired messages.
4. Check in with the person to whom you are sending messages to ensure your declaration was received and understood. Ask him to give an example from his life that illustrates the message you were trying to send.
5. Evaluate each declaration you are making, and how you are making it, to ensure that you aren't including additional messaging you are not aware of.

A few ideas to incorporate these tactics into your daily routine include simple practices such as writing down on your notepad "Don't qualify, just go," asking for feedback on your communication from trusted friends or advisors, appointing a so-called reaction buddy for yourself who can help you keep your body language in check, coming up with a mission statement or theme for the year, keeping a list of the five things that are important to you in your life front and center on your desk or mirror.

Once again, 10 ways that you can practice declaring outside of your daily routine are:

1. Practice using "I feel" statements. Emotions can often get in the way of our declarations, and using these statements gives us more practice in being aware of our emotions and engaging with them in a manner that's productive and appropriate to the situation.
2. Count the number of people who give input in a meeting before you do and ask yourself if you think that is equitable to you and to the group.
3. Write declaration segments (you don't have to share them if you don't want to) about things that you are passionate about. Be sure to include what you believe about the subject, why you believe it, how you can help further the progress toward what you want, and what makes the subject worthy of defending or evangelizing.
4. Think about things with the fill-in-the-blank statement of "If it were up to me, I would … "
5. Divide a conversation by the number of participants and ask yourself if your voice is being heard proportionally.
6. Subscribe to blogs about subjects you are confident about and that are meaningful to you. Add comments to the blog posts that give readers insight into your point of view.
7. Try creating one long sentence, or a couple of short ones, that include the components of who you are, where you are, what you want to accomplish, and why it is important.
8. Interview teammates and ask them if they know your point of view about the project you are working on together. See how close they get. If they aren't sure, it might be a

(Continued)

sign that you aren't declaring your point of view clearly enough.

9. Write down what you like about a movie and three things you would have done differently if you were the writer or director. This will help you to practice leading with the positive while being comfortable about offering your suggestions for improvements.

10. Create a meeting recap for yourself. Be clear and thorough about documenting your point of view on the content that was covered in the meeting. Then ask yourself if you think everyone who was in the meeting knows your point of view as well as it's described in the meeting recap. If not, make sure you let them know.

11

Reframing

Earl

Sorry, can't do lunch.

Erin

No worries, I needed to run some errands anyway.

Earl

Also, I have to leave early tomorrow so I won't make the client meeting.

Erin

Okay, it will be good for me to practice taking more of a lead role.

Earl

I forgot to tell you that IT let us know that the VPN will be off-line on Monday so you won't be able to work from home.

Erin

Great, I just got a new bike and needed an excuse to test it for a longer distance.

Earl

It is supposed to rain on Monday.

Erin

Looks like I won't have to wash my dirty bike, hooray!

Earl

Do you have any idea how annoying your positive attitude is?

Erin

No, but I am glad you told me because I am in the middle of a month-long self-assessment survey to help a friend who is using me as a case study for her PhD dissertation; I will note your helpful comment.

Earl

You are like Mother Teresa and Gandhi wrapped up into a young, happy, middle manager of joy, I think I may get sick .

Erin

Can I pick you up anything while I am out?

Of the Big Five, reframing feels like one of the most *physical* behaviors. Perhaps it's because when you're on stage improvising, a great way to get a new perspective on what is going on is to physically change your position in relationship to the other improvisers. Or perhaps it's because reframing is all about *seeing* the situation differently.

In the late 1980s I was fortunate enough to hear *National Geographic* photographer Dewitt Jones give a presentation that focused on the metaphor of *changing lenses*. A specific part of his presentation showed a photograph of a pinecone. He then used a different lens on the same place to reveal a pine tree, and then a *different* lens on the same place to reveal a pine forest—and finally, another lens on the same place to reveal a mountain range. It impacted me and empowered me to remember that even if we can't change the reality of the situation, we are always in control and in charge of *how we look at it*. We always have the option to choose to look at a situation differently. And that's what the process of reframing entails.

I have used reframing in both my work with clients and in my practice as an entrepreneur as a way to gain a new perspective and to find ways around obstacles. I have found it most useful when searching for a new way to accomplish a goal, even when a seemingly real obstacle presents itself and the original solution path is no longer available.

I have shared with you some of my struggles with the Big Five. While deferring judgment and listening are behaviors I have to constantly work on, I am proud of my ability to reframe. I love to play the role of chief reframer when a group of people thinks, "Well, it looks like this just isn't going to be able to work." Reframing obstacles, looking at the situation from a different angle, and finding another path toward the solution is a wonderful way to add value to any process.

In the past 15 years of participating, designing, and leading innovation and learning events, my team and I have observed that things seldom go completely according to plan. In fact, our clients often share that one of the ways we add value to their efforts is by *not* being rattled by last-minute changes, challenges, or unforeseen obstacles. The impetus for the reframing in those circumstances is the unexpected; and instead of being startled and eliminating possibilities, we rally, reinvent, and create more possibilities.

Reframing energizes me. I truly get a kick out of the challenge of finding a new way of looking at or doing something. However, I do have a piece of cautionary advice for the reframers out there. When things go completely smoothly and according to plan, I often question whether or not they are innovative enough. After years of practicing reframing, I have seen its value in the innovation process so many times that when things go without obstacle or interruption I truly miss having the opportunity to reframe a little bit. I'm sure if someone dug deep enough into my psyche there would be some proof that I even manufacture obstacles or changes to ensure that I have to reframe in any given initiative. If you are like me or work with other avid reframers, you should create opportunities within the innovation process to reframe in a productive manner that does not derail or slow it down.

Reframing is not just a way to overcome obstacles. It can also serve as an integral part of the way we approach the innovation process. Reframing is an engine that provides a diverse set of perspectives throughout the process continuously and not just when something goes wrong.

Reframing requires asking, "What if?" or "How about?" even when something is going very well. Of course, when you are innovating within a deadline you need to move forward and not constantly question and reexamine what you are doing. However, a measured dose of reframing sprinkled throughout the process keeps your mind sharp and continues to inspire you to at least explore the potential of new ideas, new flavors, or new versions of what you are currently doing.

Occasional reframing doesn't necessarily change a project's direction; however, it can improve it as it moves forward. Scheduling time for reframing at each step in the process will keep you in the mindset of discovery, as it will prevent you from becoming too rigid or blind to opportunities or potential challenges. We don't know what we don't know, so being disciplined about exploring different ways to look at the stage of development you are currently working on can help mitigate risk.

Reframing also is a great way to reinforce your current position and point of view. Think of how early ocean voyageurs had to use the stars and triangulation to guide themselves. Similarly, if we find at least two other ways to look at what we are currently doing and connect the dots between those two ways and our current point of view, we have just triangulated and reinforced where we are.

Since purchasing the Brave New Workshop in 1997 we've had to reframe how we look at our business many times. It became clear several years ago that the Internet and DVDs and Netflix and YouTube would be supplying many of our customers with the comedy they needed without ever leaving their homes—and many people go to their handhelds instead of the theater to get their comedy. So we needed to scratch our heads and find a way to be able to distribute our writers' and actors' talent and content on platforms other than live on stage. It doesn't mean that we will ever stop having wonderfully unique comedy performances on our main stage in downtown Minneapolis; we've been doing that for more than 50 years and will be doing it more than 50 years from now. It's simply that we must additionally reframe what we do so that our comedy can continue to reach people where they are and in the way that they need it formatted.

The same is true with our school of improvisation. Eighteen years ago our goal was to increase the size and depth of the improvisational community in the Twin Cities. We wanted to grow our school in a way that exposed people to the art form, give people the chance to learn how to perform, and organically grow the amount and type of improvisation in our community. The majority of our classes were therefore focused on learning and performing improvisation. And today, because of the success of that initiative, there are hundreds more improvisers and lots of other places to learn the art form of improvisation in the Twin Cities. Mission accomplished.

Now we are reframing our school to teach people how to transfer the values of improvisation to their everyday lives. Our goal is to reach

10,000 students per year; we currently are at around 300. This latest reframing drastically changes whom we serve, as well as how and where we serve those who can benefit from improvisation. Through the use of technology, a train-the-trainer licensing program, and worldwide satellite programs, we will now bring our reframed brand of improvisational education tools to a whole new audience in a whole new way.

In the past few years, I have had to gradually—though drastically— reframe how I view my role in our organization. As we've grown from 4 to more than 85 full-time and part-time employees, how I lead the company has changed a great deal. This process has given me great experience and insight into why it is sometimes so hard to reframe. When we reframe, what we need to do is frequently different than what we have been doing before, what we were comfortable with, and how we thought we ought to be.

I've struggled continually with reframing my role in the company, since it's frequently required me to stop doing things I've enjoyed doing. I am not nearly as involved in our theater's creative process as I once was and I don't get to perform improvisation or write comedy nearly as much as I used to. I am no longer involved in many of the day-to-day operational decisions of our organization. All of those were hard to let go of, both because I enjoyed many of the aspects of what I did and because, as with most people, it was simply hard to let go of control. But the reframing process helps me understand that this is what's truly best for the organization, our employees, and the customers we serve. Reframing was the mechanism I used in this instance to allow myself to let go.

Reframing as Methodology

Similarly to the other Big Five, an important aspect of reframing is that it is a specific and actionable way of behaving. Reframing gives us a really clear, simple thing to do.

Regardless of your definition of the word *innovation*, your love-hate relationship with data collection and analysis, or your bias toward a specific design or production model, there is one thing that we can all do on a daily basis and throughout the innovation process and life journey. We can simply stop and look at the current circumstance or situation, acknowledge how we are currently seeing it and what perceptions we have about it—and then force ourselves to look at it differently, from another point of view.

Then do it a second time. What is a different version of what we are looking at? How would someone else look at it? It works for people with diverse styles and modes of thinking: If you are a visual learner, you are changing the view. If you are crazy about innovative algorithms, you are switching out some variables and recalculating. If you are hands-on and tactile, you are picking up the situation from a different side and holding it up to the light.

Maybe it's simply thinking about two or three other types of customers who could benefit from your new product innovation or considering several other team members who could influence your point of view and asking how they would look at the situation. I also like simple and fun reframing techniques, such as asking what a 12-year-old would do. Or asking, if our budget were zero dollars how could we make this work?

We all know that an integral part of scientific research is to make sure that we have a constant and some variables. This reframing behavior simply gives us a practical way to infuse that methodology into idea generation, solution creation, and the process that gets us from wondering how we can do something to getting it done in an innovative way.

And while we're looking at this through the lens of science—if we reframe throughout the innovation process we are also continually adding to the diversity of information in the innovation equation. I have seen folks spend lots of time brainstorming at the top of the process, which gives them a broad perspective on what could be done. But they then choose a set of solutions and immediately go, heads down, into executing them. It seems as though they're choosing what they think *should be* the outcome of the process before they even begin. They initially brainstormed a diverse set of ideas but used a narrow and limited process to get to the solution. If we can reframe consistently throughout the prototyping, refinement, and delivery and execution parts of the process, we're more assured of diversity of thought—and therefore of greater richness and depth in innovation.

Working with human-centered design thinkers, such as healthcare innovator Ryan Armbruster, has confirmed those notions. Design thinking has taught me that often we begin the innovation process without even knowing if we're solving for the correct issue. That methodology allows space for reframing after we have had a chance to get to know the viewpoints of the people for whom we are designing a solution. As a result, we can create innovation that is closely linked to the user's point of view and need.

Reframing Mistakes

A psychological bias called *functional fixedness* highlights our tendency to limit our view of the use of an object to its traditional use. For instance, we see a paper clip as a simple gadget designed to hold pages together, rather than something that can be reshaped and used to pick a lock. This propensity makes reframing a challenging behavior. Since innovation is clearly an iterative process—which also often borrows concepts from other fields and repurposes ideas and concepts in new contexts—the ability to reframe is critical to increasing our innovation fitness.

There is a specific application of our reframing muscles that is a hot topic in many of our client organizations. How we perceive and treat mistakes and so-called failures in the context of innovation is crucial to developing teams and individuals willing and able to innovate on a daily basis. The finding that no one likes to be wrong isn't surprising. But how we view our mistakes can be.

There are countless stories from scientists, entrepreneurs, and corporate leaders that illustrate alleged mistakes being turned into successes. From Röntgen and the X-ray to Greatbatch and the pacemaker to Fleming and penicillin, making mistakes is part of innovation lore, part of learning, and part of progress. It is also part of our natural world. Think about the way evolution works: Apparent mistakes in DNA produce the variances that allow different species and features to evolve.

Mistakes can also be tragic, full of consequences and heartbreak. So how do we create a healthy balance of mistake prevention and celebration? One way is to reframe mistakes into learning opportunities, and instead of focusing solely on what happened, why it happened, and who is responsible, asking what did we learn and how will what happened affect our behavior and the way we do things moving forward. That attitude does not undermine the severity of the mistake and its possible negative effects, but helps us find something *useful* and move forward.

The other way to reframe our relationship with mistakes is to create space and time when mistakes don't have dire consequences. That is especially important for innovation activities. Simulations, games, improv exercises, and role playing are all mechanisms through which we can play out scenarios, make mistakes, have fun with those mistakes, learn from them, and reframe them into useful insights and ideas.

As someone who confesses to having made lots of mistakes and having learned a lot through trial and error, FINNEGANS CEO Jacquie Berglund has a very insightful way to look at mistakes: "In life, there are so many important and necessary detours," she says. "I call them important and necessary. I don't believe in regret. Whether it's a wrong turn on a business idea, or even a marriage, I'm really glad for and will gladly take all of those important necessary detours. They made me who I am today and I'm going to be a more effective leader and a more effective human being, and maximize my potential, because of all that stuff. Why on earth would I want to do it any quicker than I did? I really wouldn't."

APPLICATION EXAMPLE: REFRAMING

Some days, I think it must be odd for my sons to have a professional speaker and trainer as a dad. I've heard them answer the question "What does your dad do?" with "He owns a comedy theater and talks a lot." Certainly not untrue. But there are days when I am really touched that the work my wife and I do bleeds into our personal life and influences our sons to at least contemplate things that have to do with improving the human condition and helping people become their best selves. A particular Sunday was one of them.

My older son, William, and I decided to spend the morning together, just he and I. We went downtown and walked through the theater, checked on how the construction was going on a new building we had just bought across the street, and then went to brunch. He was 11 at the time. It was great—lots of conversation: questions from me about school and friends and sports, questions

(Continued)

from him about the new building, what it was like when Mom and I were first dating, what I talked about in my speeches, and what my job was all about.

I told him about the mindset of discovery and the Big Five behaviors that we practice. He wanted to know about the fear side of things, too. He was very interested in why people would not share ideas and why they might be afraid to be as innovative as they could. I shared some examples of the things that might go on in the workplace. Things such as the meeting-after-the-meeting, when people who have chosen not to share ideas in a meeting share them with a smaller group at happy hour, or times when people don't share ideas that they think are out-there when their boss is in the room because they're afraid their boss might think less of them. He was taking it in and I could see the wheels in his head moving pretty fast.

After a great morning downtown we got back in the car and took the roughly 25-minute journey to see Mom and Michael. As soon as we were on the freeway William shared an amazingly simple and wise tool that he had created. He said that in the morning homeroom discussions at school, the teacher had been leading a talk about how we can't always choose the circumstances in our lives, but we can always choose our reactions. He said that he had been practicing this tool he had invented to help with his reactions, and he thought it might help the people I gave speeches to react to new ideas and situations so that they could be as innovative as they could. He also told me that he thought everybody should be as innovative as they could be, because that is the only way we were going to figure out how to cure cancer, end hunger, and keep all the water on the planet safe for drinking. The name of the tool he invented? The *reaction fraction*.

The reaction fraction, he explained, is a way to help people decide how to react to new things that happen in their lives. They can also use it to understand whether the reaction they had was the right one.

The reaction fraction is made up of a numerator and a denominator, just like any other fraction. But in this case, the parts of the fraction represent things that happen to us and how we react. It looks like this:

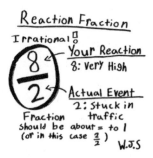

The denominator (the number on the bottom, for those of you who are out of practice!) is composed of new things that happen to us. These are new ideas that come our way, or circumstances we experience. The numerical value of the denominator is based on how big of a deal the idea or event is. So, if something big happens—such as getting engaged or winning the lottery or having a baby—that may be a 9 or a 10. But if you win a card game or get some ice cream or do well on a spelling test that might be a 2 or a 3. The same holds true for sad things: Losing a parent may be a 9 and losing a Little League game might be a 2.

The numerator is the one we get to *choose*, William explained; it represents the reaction we have or choose to have when this new thing comes our way. We also assign a numerical value to our reaction. Smiling and saying thank you might be a 2; jumping up and down and screaming might be a 9. Once again, he said, it can also apply to sad things; if we are a little sad or upset that might be a 2 or 3, and if we are really crying a lot that might be a 9.

The goal, as William explained it, is to choose a reaction that is *close to the numerical value of the circumstance*—that is, for the numerator be the same as the denominator so that the value of the fraction is as close to 1 as possible. When the reaction is the same number as the circumstances we know that we reacted the right way. If it's much too low or much too high, it's an indication that we need to choose a different reaction.

(*Continued*)

He cited some examples to highlight his point: If you were stuck in traffic, you should try for a fraction of 2/2, but if your dog died, it's okay to have a reaction fraction of 9/9.

I learn a lot from my sons each day—but this was an exceptional lesson. I hope Williams's reaction fraction can help you.

Reframing Fitness Plan and Workouts

All right—here we go again. We have broken down reframing into several "muscles" you can exercise and have distilled a few tactics you can employ immediately to become a master reframer.

Muscles to Exercise

1. Break down ideas and circumstances into their parts.
2. Identify your point of view on ideas and circumstances.
3. Identify and take into account emotions that might be coloring your perceptions.
4. Distill the essence of what you are trying to accomplish.
5. Find what's useful in ideas and circumstances; discard the rest.

Tactics to Practice

1. Ground yourself in a feeling of gratitude before you tackle a challenge. Literally *say* thank you before you begin.
2. Create a few profiles of typical customers or collaborators and use their lens when you problem solve. For example, "How would Becky look at this?" "What would this mean to Ashish?" And so on.
3. Include reframing time in your processes.
4. Seek out insight into different fields, industries, and ways of working.
5. Fail in a safe environment and move forward.

A few ideas to incorporate these tactics into your daily routine include simple practices such as keeping images around you that ground you in gratitude, scheduling reframing sessions with your team or by yourself (make it a regular part of meetings to continually bring in fresh ideas), inviting your customers and users to share their insights regularly, consuming media that gives you insights into various fields, and taking classes in various arts, sports, and skills you know you will fail in.

And here are 10 things you can add to your reframing fitness plan:

1. Ask, "How could we complete this if we had no budget?"
2. Try to come up with three different answers to the same question—all of which are correct.
3. Try to find, and then listen to, five different versions of the same song. For example, a country version of a Beatles song is the same song, but it sounds a lot different.
4. Make a list of 10 things that ended up much differently—and actually, better—than you expected.
5. Go into the garage and find an item, then think of 10 things it could be used for besides the use it was designed for (e.g., tires make great playground swings!).
6. Write a couple of alternate endings for a movie or book and see which one you like the best.
7. Plan a fictional vacation with three very different people you know and see how each version of a great vacation differs.
8. List all the major technology in your life (e.g., car, computer, phone, electricity, refrigeration, etc.) and then find solutions to the challenges that would come up in your day from losing each of them. For instance, if I didn't have a car I would take the bus or carpool.

(Continued)

9. Try to list benefits of losing something you consider to be a positive aspect of your life. If I didn't have an e-mail account, for instance, I would have more good conversations with people.

10. When planning a leisure activity, consider what you want to do, what you don't want to do, what someone else would want to do, and a new activity that you have never tried or thought of doing.

12

Jumping In

Mark

Have you decided?

Renee

No. I've tried but there are just so many factors to consider.

Mark

I know, right? Like what if you don't like it after the first few minutes?

Renee

Right. Once you make your choice, there's no turning back.

Mark

I am not even sure how it will end.

Renee

Good point. The last thing you need is another surprise when it comes to romance.

Mark

I know a few people who have experience with it and it seems like not everyone thought it was right for them.

Renee

It is also a major time commitment.

Mark

Good point. If I am going to commit to that much time I need to know I will get something out of it.

Renee

I hate this. Why can't these types of things be more clear?

Mark

You are really stressing about this.

Renee

I know. I think I am just going to wait.

Mark

Good call. It will be in the theaters for at least a few more weeks.

Renee

Yep — and there's always Netflix.

I have heard many descriptions of what it feels like to begin an improvisational comedy scene: jumping off the cliff into the dark abyss, hang gliding with no hang glider, entering a mystical and imaginary world full of wonder and possibility. I guess those are pretty good, but the reality is a little less dramatic: One person typically walks forward and begins to speak. Most improv scenes start with a small movement or word, which leads to the next one and the next one, and three minutes later you realize, not only did we start—we're already finished.

I don't mean to minimize how wonderful it is to begin a great improv scene; it can be full of exhilarating unknowns and wide-open possibility, but for our purposes and from a much more practical point of view, it simply begins.

That's what jumping in means. Just begin.

There is some value in taking the grandeur out of starting. I've asked a lot of people about why they won't start something—and for many of them, it's because they are turning a single small step into a big, hairy, risk-filled, life-changing decision. I've noticed that we can associate that single step of beginning with all of the possible rights and wrongs that could happen after it. Perhaps that's why we unjustifiably put so much pressure on that first moment. We are not really afraid of the first moment; it's all of the things that could happen *after that* that we are hesitating about. Like the ski jumper at the top of the jump, we have convinced ourselves that once we begin, ideas or decisions or responsibilities or whatever are going to cascade and avalanche and accelerate. And perhaps that makes us feel out of control. We want to wait until we can really know what can happen in that second and third and fourth and thousandth moment after we start.

The truth is that we always feel better once we begin. The ideas start to flow, we get a clear understanding of what we need to do, and we're less frozen. As a matter of fact, much of my work with teams that are trying to innovate better has to do with keeping the team members engaged and the energy of the process high. Ironically, we're often scared that if we begin, things will get too full of energy and too out of hand too fast, but things rarely get out of hand. They usually slow down and get a bit boring, to the point that we have to create systems and reminders to increase the pace and keep up the energy.

To jump in can mean a lot of different things depending on our roles, the projects we are working on, or what task we are accomplishing on any given day. It could be as simple as making a decision or voicing your intention. It could involve stepping up and volunteering to collaborate, or taking on a leadership role on a team that is designing a solution. It may mean that you're learning a new technology or agreeing to widen your job responsibility. It may be investigating options, or trying something that seems outside your comfort zone, or partnering on a project with someone you don't know very well. It may be the commitment to strengthen a relationship with a client or work with a new set of customers. It is beginning. It is the *opposite* of hesitating. And some days, it is hard.

Part of the reason it is hard is because staying in information-collection mode is safe. Our perception of risk can deter us from action, because action brings unpredictable circumstances. Once we begin, we are on a slippery slope that may include confusing information, others' points of view, not enough time, not enough clarity, and, oh my goodness, emotion!

Action demands we make decisions. Decisions we are held accountable for or which impact people around us, our organizations, our goals. So it is not a surprise that fear can show its ugly head when we have to begin. Hiding behind data and spending resources on over-analysis is one way that many professionals address that fear, although it is not the most effective way.

Psychologist Gerd Gigerenzer has dedicated his career to studying decision making. His research shows that 50 percent of all decisions in a business are so-called gut decisions, although they are never publicly named as such. He argues that the tendency to attempt to make decisions solely on the basis of statistics and algorithms is sound in a stable world, but in the highly unpredictable world we live in, intuition and smart heuristics are valuable tools to respond to quick changes and uncertainty. Managers already rely on intuition (an "unconscious form of knowledge") but waste significant amount of organizational time defending their decisions with data in case they turn out to be wrong (Gigerenzer 2014).

Wouldn't it make more sense to help employees become more in touch with their instincts and exercise them when appropriate so that they can make better decisions and, more importantly, end the convenient stalling technique of analysis paralysis? We think so.

That's why taking action, beginning, or jumping in is a key behavior for innovation, which pursues or creates something new that is completely uncertain. The only way we will be able to know what to do next is to *begin doing something*. We can gain a significant amount of insight and information through the process of moving forward—whether that involves idea generation or prototyping or sketching or having a conversation. To do nothing will generate no new insights or clues as to what is next.

Once we jump in we open a spigot to allow a flow of ideas, circumstances, insights, and data completely new and separate from what we could manufacture in our heads. In the second we begin, experiential data gives us a much more human, and perhaps customer-focused, set of insights because it is created by the interactive, iterative, and energizing movement forward. It shows up as things we learn in conversations, things we experience on our feet, things that came from ideas bounced off someone else, and things that were made clear through fatigue and frustration and excitement.

It seems so obvious—yet we often fool ourselves into thinking that if we just study, analyze, and mind-map enough we can figure out the best solution. Of course, this is ridiculous. Think of the difference between learning about and analyzing the facts compared to experiencing the very same content you are intellectualizing. You can study sailing as much as you want, but there isn't a book or video in the world that will give you the same sensation as moving through the water with the power of the wind. You can listen to as many albums as you want and the experience will never compare to the live concert.

And you can read every parenting magazine article you can get your hands on and it still won't completely prepare you for that first week with your first child. You've got to jump into that sailboat, jump into that mosh pit, and jump into that diaper!

Jumping in, in itself, is actually a wonderful distraction that can *reduce* our fear. If we just begin, we no longer spend as much time or energy worrying about if we *ought to* begin. After you jump in, your fear is replaced by the focus and energy needed to move forward with the task at hand. My wife, for example, is very kind and often describes how her relationship with me has helped her reduce her fear of jumping in.

She often explains it to others in this way: "Hundreds of times in our marriage I have realized that it would be ridiculous for me to worry about whether or not I should be doing the next exciting thing we have planned, because somehow he has helped me to start and we have been doing that very same activity for several minutes already!" She always tends to give me a specific look in those situations. Some of the looks I remember the most were when we were a hundred feet into our zip-line trip, or already launched for our Navy SEALs-style whale-watching trip, or both yelling "Mush!" to the sled dogs on a 20-degrees-below-zero day. I love being too busy doing something to worry about whether or not we ought to.

Of course, you don't want to be overly reckless or impulsive. But at some point, the research and groundwork has to be finished—and we have to have achieved a healthy balance between trust in the data and trust in our instincts.

Listening to the Itch

One person who is very much in touch with her instincts and has followed them throughout her life and career is Jacquie Berglund, whom we've been featuring throughout the book. Jacquie's career has gone through several 180-degree turns, and all because of her endless confidence that when she jumps in, she will figure out the best way to move forward and innovate.

John:　Talk about times when you either didn't have enough information, you didn't have enough funding, or you didn't have enough experience.

Jacquie: Sweeney, it's my life. Everything I've done is like that.

John: Think of the average person reading this book. Maybe she's in middle management. She's trying to do the next best thing but she doesn't have enough data. She doesn't know if her budget's perfect. She's hesitant.

In our world, you've got 15 percent of what you need and your gut's screaming at you—so you go, right? What were some milestones at FINNEGANS that you look back at it and say, "How did I have the guts to do this?"

Jacquie: Actually, the first example I have of that happened before FINNEGANS. It's about listening to that inner voice. At college I was an idealist; I really wanted to change the world. I got a job at a local search-firm network. I did really well; I worked there three years. I had all these big accounts but I started to get this inner-itch, as I call it.

I'm making all this money at my age, right out of college. But I felt something happening inside and kept asking, "Why am I not happy? I work with awesome people at a great company." This was the beginning of my journey of listening to that voice inside.

Throughout my career that voice has gotten louder and I listen to it more quickly. So I took a day off from work, went over to the library, and checked out study-abroad programs. I said, "That's what I need. I need to go back to school. I need to be inspired again—I've lost the inspiration." I found one for a Master of Arts program in Paris. I immediately said, "I'm going there."

I decided I was going to go global and help poor countries develop. I applied and got accepted. I sold everything I had and packed up a suitcase. I didn't speak French and I didn't know a soul over there. I have no idea what I was thinking.

It was the hardest year of my life. I got there and thought to myself, "What have I done?" They were so mean to me. I ran out of money. Yet I ended up staying for seven years. I'm a believer that if you're doing the right thing and you take the risk, you get the support. I applied for an internship at the OECD, the Organisation for Economic Co-operation and Development. It is the best model of development assistance in the history of the world. I got the internship. My French is the worst—I can't think of a good reason I got hired.

After that I ended up just getting these consultancies for seven years and I moved up. This was in the 1990s when Russia was breaking up and I was in the most entrepreneurial group in the OECD, which was helping to train government officials in the northern regions of Russia on market economics.

So here I am with this really cool job, doing all this dynamic stuff. But after five years I started to get this itch again. I thought, "Okay, wait a minute; this was my dream job. I thought this was going to be my career."

John: Were you helping people?

Jacquie: It was really at the policy level. I thought, "The real work is getting done at the grassroots level. I want to be down there. I want to be getting my hands dirty." And I wasn't. Also, back then I didn't know I was an entrepreneur. I would say, "Okay, I have this great idea. I think we should ... " And I was told, "You need to simmer down. There are no changing things here." That started to drive me crazy.

John: Were you frustrated with the speed of implementation?

Jacquie: Yeah. There was no ideation. Nobody took me seriously. I felt like nobody thought I had a good idea in my head and I thought I did. So I got the itch again. I ended up moving back to the United States. My good friend Kieran Folliard was opening an Irish restaurant and I needed back surgery; I had degenerative disc disease. I didn't have any health insurance when I moved back, and Kieran said, "Jacquie, come work for me. I'll get you health insurance; you're going to be my director of marketing."

I said, "Well, Kieran, I've never worked at a bar or restaurant a day in my life. I was poli-sci/communications major, I had Marketing 101. I don't know if I'm really qualified." He said, "You're going to be great."

John: And—you weren't going to be able to work for the six months you were recovering from back surgery.

Jacquie: Right. Again, I was jumping into a job where I felt, "This is a little scary." I remember going to Barnes & Noble and buying marketing books and thinking, "Okay, I have to try and figure this out."

My poor parents were saying, "Here's Jacquie at the OECD in Paris. Now she's working at an Irish pub in Minneapolis. She went and got her master's degree so she could work at an Irish pub." They were just beside themselves. But Kieran and I started working together and had a blast. I got the back surgery, got that all sorted out. Then I got this itch—for the third time now. But this time I listened to it more quickly.

John: And that was how you started FINNEGANS.

Jacquie: Right. There were three things that surfaced around the same time: The CFO for the pubs was complaining that Kieran and I were donating too much of our marketing budget with no strategic-giving plan, a friend of mine mentioned that Kieran was such a local celebrity that he could have his own beer with his picture on it, and I heard Billy Shore, the founder of Share our Strength, speak and talk about having a for-profit company fund nonprofit activities. I was taking a bubble bath—where I do my best thinking—and I thought, "What if we create our own beer company and we give all the profits back to one cause? I think we could kill it with this thing." I pitched the idea to Kieran and he said, "You're nuts." But then he said, "Okay."

That's how the whole thing started. I said, "Kieran, if we really want to make a difference, we got to have this in every pub in Minnesota, not just yours." I wrote him a check for a dollar for the rights to the beer brand and we changed the name to FINNEGANS. Then in September 2000 I jumped off that cliff to go run the beer company. I did no research. I knew nothing about beer, or selling beer.

John: It seems as if that model of the all-proceeds-go-to-charity beer company giving has taken care of your itch for at least 15 years.

Jacquie: Yeah, but I've got it again now.

John: You call it your itch, or your voice. I think that it's the call of service.

Jacquie: It's the meaning piece. For 15 years, I've had great meaning in my work. I've never lasted in a job more than 5 years so this is huge for me. And now I'm jumping in again.

If there's a theme in everything I've done, it's that I have no training. Now I'm starting a FINNovation Lab, a sort of incubator for social entrepreneurs. I am not exactly sure what that looks like yet. But we're going to go do it. Because it seems like we're building the pieces to make that happen.

John: You also don't need it to be something yet. You just need it to *be*, and you're learning about what it *could be*, right? Which is different than knowing everything? I feel some days there's a privilege or a benefit in not knowing everything.

Jacquie: Oh, I think there is a huge benefit—that openness and that that whole sense of discovery. Every project I've ever done, I start there. I look at stuff, connect dots, and it usually ends up being something that nobody's done before.

Although I have known Jacquie for almost 20 years, I didn't have all the early details of her innovative path. I have been struck by how many of the courageous innovators I have met have had such absolutely unpredictable paths. And yet at the same time most all of them have had a very clear and defined sense of what drives them and what they are ultimately trying to accomplish. It started for Jacquie in her teens; she somehow gained a very clear sense of how she would lead a life well lived. She evaluated the results of her day by whether or not she improved the community in which she lived. As broad as that seems, you can tell that it is very clear, and very specific to her. She knows who she is and she knows what she wants to get done.

Sister Super

Sometimes there is wonderful and perhaps divine serendipity in a person's name that also serves as a description of who or how they are. Sr. Dolores Super, OSB, is super in many ways. Super smart, super funny, super educated, super energized—superhuman, perhaps.

Sr. Dolores came from very modest means; she grew up in a family of 11 children in small-town, depression-era beginnings. Her life journey could be a book all to itself. Leaving home to attend high school at St. Benedict's in St. Joseph, Minnesota, at the age of 16, she took with her the strong and mighty sense of feminism that she saw every day in her mother. First the high school degree, then the undergrad, then the formation and commitment to be a member of the Sisters of the Order of Saint Benedict, the largest Benedictine community in the United States. At its peak in the 1950s, the monastery had 1,278 fully professed sisters who were ministering in more than 80 schools and healthcare organizations, as well as numerous other ministries.

Throughout her life and career she was asked to pursue educational or professional opportunities that she had never even dreamed of. She will be the first to tell you that despite a world-class pursuit and study of music, she never considered herself to be very talented at it. That didn't matter; there was a need for her to go beyond her own perception of her talents, for her to go beyond her own comfort zone, for her to jump in.

It would be a great story if it ended there; however, her next career steps took her even further out of her comfort zone. In 1984, despite having no background in health care, Sr. Super was asked to serve on the St. Cloud (Minnesota) Hospital board as chair. She served 10 years in that position and 9 years with CentraCare and Queen of Peace Hospital in New Prague, Minnesota. In the early 1990s the Catholic Health Association asked Super to testify in Washington, DC, before a Senate subcommittee, pleading the case of the uninsured for added healthcare assistance.

It might seem like a bit of a jump to go from a career in music to being the chairperson of the board of a hospital that's now a part of the second largest health system in the state of Minnesota. But again, Sr. Dolores Super simply said yes.

I've tried to apply her ability to jump in to my own life. If there is an opportunity for me to do something different that will serve others, and I am hesitant, or unsure, or frightened, I have a simple process for figuring out what to do next. I ask one question: What would Sr. Super do?

Sr. Super: I could play the organ, but I never thought I was any good at music. As a young sister I was told, "You're going to major in music." You know, obedience was so important. I was 18 years old. What could I say? I'm not musical? I thought, well, let's see: If I major in music I'll probably go to a parish. There are a lot of parishes that our sisters are at. People won't know that I can't play. I'll pretend. I can do that. Then I taught for a few years.

Then the prioress came one day and she said, "You're going to go to graduate school. Now, you find the best music school in the country." Well, obedient. Right? I look around and it's Indiana University, best music school in the country. I apply there and I get accepted and I thought, "Oh, now they're going to find out!" I was just petrified when I got there, but I at least found out that other students were petrified, too. I thought, "I can't do this." Lack of confidence in my musical ability just plagued me. What did I do? I majored in music.

When I got back, they said, "You'll teach in the music department." "Okay, I thought, I'll get into it, and I can learn more." I had taught one year and the chair of the music department was appointed academic dean. The prioress said to me, "You will now be chair of the music department." I thought, "My God in heaven, now what am I going to do?"

We come from a long line of strong women, both in my family—my mother and my sisters—but also the sisters in my community. I thought, "Well, okay. I can do that, too. I can be chair."

Later our prioress asked that some sisters consider shifting into administration and I thought, "I can do that." I left the music department, completed an internship with a college in Kansas City, and moved into academic administration and eventually became the academic dean.

John: Are you skipping a little part about running a hospital?

Sr. Super: Our prioress, who headed a committee that selected the chair of the St. Cloud Hospital board, met with me one day and told me, "We'd like you to be chair of the board." I said, "I don't know anything about health care—nothing, zip. If I have a headache, I know what to do, but the chair of the hospital board? This is not an insignificant institution." She said, "Well, you think about it." So I did.

This really is the reason I took it. I thought, "I'm 53 years old. How many more opportunities like this would I have to learn a whole new discipline?" I went to the prioress and I said, "Tell me a little bit more about why you chose me, because this is out of the blue." She said, "Well, you run a good meeting. You know how to listen. I've heard you—you know how to synthesize things, bring them together, and you help people to make a decision. I've seen you do that. You're smart. The rest you can learn." The rest you can learn?

John: But you did, didn't you? And you made an impact.

Sr. Super: I knew that we had to establish a clinic for people without insurance, especially women. Single women with children living in this area who had no insurance. It was morally right.

I raised the issue and heard, "We can't afford it." I said, "We cannot *not* afford it."

John: And you made it happen.

Sr. Super: When I come to the Heavenly Gate and St. Peter says, "How did you get here?" I'll say, "Mid-Minnesota Clinic."

John: I don't see you fret about the unpredictability of your next day, let alone your next career. You have this calmness.

Sr. Super: You know what that's called in our life? Stability. We take a promise of stability. It's not only to be rooted in a place but to be rooted in a life. To be rooted in values, that's what stability is all about. And it works. How do I know that? I watch the young come in that haven't been in long and they're scared. We all understand that. But once you get really rooted, it's easier. It's easier to say yes.

John: We've done lots of research centered on why people won't come up with new ideas or take new risks in a corporate setting. I thought it would be because of budget restrictions or legal restrictions. But it was all because of self-doubt and fear.

Sr. Super: Do you know what you should do? Everybody in their background has an aunt or an uncle or a grandmother—it's often the grandmother—who truly was a pillar for them. Have them recall that person. What would that person say to you? It's amazing what you can do if you recall, and recalling that, you bring that person right into the room. That gives you courage.

What a joy it was to spend time with Sister Super, especially since our conversation happened at the monastery in Sophia House, the house where she lives. It's a place where you'll find many octogenarians with the energy levels of thirty-something hipsters—and Sister Super is certainly one of them. Her eyes are bright, her smile is contagious, and she can barely contain herself in telling you the next story of how one of the sisters taught her something marvelous.

For a person who has accomplished as much as she has—becoming a teacher and an administrator, and a healthcare leader whose innovations are still being modeled—she is completely without ego. She will be the first to tell you she has claimed her gifts as a fine organist and that she finds much joy in her daily early-morning hour of organ practice as well as in playing for community liturgical services. She spends much of her time in the archives learning about and then organizing and sharing the stories of the hundreds of amazing sisters that have gone before her. She relayed countless examples and stories of how the Benedictine women were strong and innovative—against ridiculous obstacles like Napoleon's forces in Bavaria or in the simple ways they help each other with career and life decisions. It was clear that the Benedictine culture, created by repetitive, simple, and daily adherence to particular practices, was what she gave credit to.

That strong and powerful influence was how she was able to say yes to opportunities in her life that most of us would've run from as fast as we could.

Jumping in to Serve

We talked in Chapter 6 about how the attitude of serving others can help us ground ourselves in the mindset of discovery. That same attitude of service is especially effective when it comes to practicing the behavior of jumping in.

In March 2014 we hosted a screening of the film *The Starfish Throwers* at our event center. It is a beautiful film that documents the amazing work of three generous people who are doing small things each day to feed the hungry. It was created by my friend Jesse Roesler, who hoped the film would create a ripple effect of goodness as it affects those who watch it.

It certainly did that for me. One of the three people the film features is Mr. Allen Law, a teacher working in the heart of Minneapolis's underserved neighborhoods and public schools. Law's so-called retirement has involved 15 years of spending every night driving his van through the city's streets handing out sandwiches, socks, mittens, and bus tokens to the hungry and homeless. And I do mean *every night*; Law has missed fewer than 10 nights in 15 years and has not slept in his own bed during that period. He has 19 freezers in his apartment where he stores the sandwiches that are made by local groups who want to help. In 2015 he will hand out more than 1 million sandwiches. He spends almost every moment of his life in the mind set of discovery.

About the same time that I was getting to know Mr. Law, my friend Jacquie Berglund was implementing a new idea for her social entrepreneurship beer company, FINNEGANS. It's called the Reverse Food Truck, and while it looks like any other food truck, people bring food to it instead of buying food from it. Jacquie's amazing army of volunteers then brings the food to distribution centers, which feed our community's hungry citizens.

Instead of simmering in envy or passively appreciating the amazing idea my friend had, I jumped in.

First I made a list of some of the most common things that people in many countries do on a regular basis. I knew that the biggest obstacle for many people in helping others is the fact that they are just too busy. So I set out to reframe and find a way to allow people to help others without the need to carve out additional time or go to another location. Not too far down on my list of common activities came happy hour. Asia does it, Europe does it, and the Americas certainly do it. So what could we do to have people continue to go to happy hour as usual but make it different so that it benefits the community?

I asked myself, what do people do at happy hour? They drink. That's pretty good, especially if they're drinking FINNEGANS, which donates all of its proceeds to the hungry. They connect with others; I'm a big fan of that. They complain about work. Well, I don't like that, it doesn't help anybody. Bingo, we found what we could replace; we reframed happy hour.

We simply take a normal happy hour, host it at our event center, serve FINNEGANS beer, and park the Reverse Food Truck underneath the marquee on the busiest street in Minneapolis. Instead of sitting around complaining about how our bosses don't understand our definition of life balance, we make sandwiches together. For Mr. Law. For the hungry in our community. That's Happy Hour Squared.

When we first vetted the idea internally and externally, we heard lots of great things that would make Happy Hour Squared a great success. Many of them would also have taken lots of time to get done. "Before we begin, we should create a web site and a Facebook page" and "We should figure out exactly how the room should be set up to optimize the sandwich making" or "We need to have a social media campaign before we can start." Others were: "We should clearly figure out exactly how many sandwiches we can make, but to do that, we'll need to know how many people are going to show up." "We should figure out how often we should have a Happy Hour Squared, but that will depend on how many people might show up." "We should create a logo and try to get some press and develop a PR campaign." These were great ideas, but what we really needed to do was decide to make

2,000 sandwiches the third Thursday of every month come hell or high water until we had made 1 million sandwiches.

And that's what we did; we just began. We didn't really know how it would go, and we certainly didn't have all we needed. We had hardly any of it figured out. But so far, as of June 2015, we've made 35,000 sandwiches, gotten a Facebook page, gotten some great press, created a website—and accomplished it all because we just jumped in. Next we want to figure out how to scope and scale the idea so we can have 1 million locations that each make 1 million sandwiches. So if you have any ideas, let us know at www.happyhoursquared.com.

Jiggly Boy

In 2003, as a way to increase engagement at the Minnesota Timberwolves NBA basketball games, I was asked to create and portray a super fan who would dance in front of 16,000 people at the game with his shirt off. It was not something I immediately wanted to do. It's a long and complicated story, but I jumped in, I danced—and the next thing I knew we were all over the news, on ESPN's *SportsCenter* and on the *Today* show, twice. Kevin Garnett was the star player on the Timberwolves at the time. It ended up being a lot of fun, and in hindsight I was really glad I jumped in—despite the fact that I was now relatively well-known in our community as… Jiggly Boy!

Fast-forward almost 12 years, to February 2015, with the unlikely and impossible-to-predict return of Kevin Garnett to the Minnesota Timberwolves after playing for both the Celtics and the Nets. We decided to bring the character back, this time joined by two fly boys, who happened to be our 11-year-old and 9-year-old sons. The return of Jiggly Boy was to take place on the first night that Kevin Garnett played back in Minnesota. There was a packed house, along with a huge amount of energy and press coverage.

Everything went as planned, and both the boys and I certainly jumped in. After I had removed my shirt and revealed the words "Welcome back KG" on my chest, the stadium went nuts. Much to my surprise, Kevin Garnett himself—having just come out of the huddle for the timeout—turned and looked me straight in the eye. He then smiled—and the place exploded! This time, thanks to the Internet and this new phenomenon called "going viral," Jiggly Boy went from local funny guy to worldwide YouTube personality. As of July 2015, we'd gotten almost 7 million views on YouTube alone with five times that number worldwide. But the jumping in was just beginning. As soon as we reached 1 million hits, which was in less than a week, I knew that we had something—and I also knew that we had to *do* something. Things like this don't come along too often, and you need to act fast, and gain as much from them as possible.

I started looking at photographs from that night and saw Kevin Garnett's huge smile, my sons' smiles of excitement, and all the people around us with their phones out and their smiles on! Something about smiles was clearly in the mix. I knew that I wanted to use this ridiculous level of being noticed to help someone. So I started asking my network, and a friend told me about Smile Network International. It's a locally run national nonprofit that does miraculous work worldwide on missions that provide cleft palate and lip surgery to children who cannot afford them. They literally *create smiles*.

I know it was time to jump in. Because of the generosity of our small but strong volunteer team, we were able to have www.jigglyboy .com up and running in 48 hours. Press releases were sent out, interviews were done, and before long we were actively raising money on the website for Smile Network International. At the website, you can view the video, create a customized meme, shop for Jiggly Boy merchandise (all proceeds get donated), and most importantly, with one click of a button, donate directly to Smile Network International.

I'm quite sure we didn't do it exactly how we should have. We certainly could have spent more time, and figured out the perfect way to launch our new endeavor. But we got it done fast, and it's improving each day as we learn. The bottom line: We started raising thousands of dollars to bring smiles to children right away. Please go to www .jigglyboy.com and donate to help a child smile. Sometimes jumping in feels really, really good!

Barriers to Jumping into Innovation

We consider ourselves to be very lucky. We get to work with fantastic clients who want to do the right thing and make their companies engines for innovation and progress. We are fortunate to be able to interact with and learn from very smart, driven, and passionate people, who are in the trenches of the battle for innovation, and who have to constantly make the choice between fear and discovery. What they tell us and what we witness at their organizations has convinced us that it is not easy to be an innovation athlete. In fact, there are some real barriers to jump into behaving innovatively. And while some of these obstacles are inherent in organizations' systems and processes, they can have very real behavioral consequences. We have highlighted a few of the obstacles we hear about most often.

Barrier 1: Status

Status is a real deal. Most mid-size and large companies have organizational charts set up as a hierarchy—an architecture that seems to almost manufacture status. People spend a significant amount of time knowing who's above and below, what career paths make sense or don't, who has influence and who can help them with leverage and getting things done. That part makes sense: Getting things done is why we sign up for our jobs and love what we do. However, it can also put up some barriers to behaving as an innovation athlete.

Status can incite fear when it is not treated properly. I've seen many ideation sessions hum along and produce interesting and disruptive ideas until a team leader shows up. At the moment that this person appears, the tone and energy of the room changes and the work loses some of its edge and spark. Sometimes that can be a substantiated result of the leader's behavior, but more often than not it is a natural, subconscious toning down on the team's part.

I don't have the answer to overcoming the barrier of status. But I can at least offer a few observations and hints about it.

I am a big advocate of creating a *culture of one*. We can combat the vertical nature of the org chart and its inherent hierarchy of status by studying our own behaviors and deciding to be culture co-creators; that is, we can actively establish a culture in every interaction, every conference call, every meeting we have. That culture of one will affect others. Humans are social beings who are wired to imitate each other without even knowing it. Our brains have mirror neurons, which make it possible to transmit our emotions and behaviors. So if a culture defined by status can grow, so can a culture of discovery.

Another strategy you can use to decrease the impact of status is listening, which can be used whether you are the person with a higher or a lower status. Listening is a great equalizer. If you have a higher status, listen to those you lead. When people feel heard it is easier for them to relate to you as a peer, which will temper status organically.

If you are a person with lower status, listen well to get to know the person (organizationally) above you. We often make incorrect assumptions about what the person we report to thinks or feels. As you get to know him, connect, and listen for ways to build a relationship of respect and equality. That will help break down the plaque that status builds up.

Even if you're not able to authentically connect with the person of higher status, listening is still a great way to show respect. Everyone wants to feel as if people are really hearing them—and if, unfortunately, someone is using her status as leverage to gain power, perhaps she is just asking to be heard, albeit in an unproductive manner.

Barrier 2: Time

It is vital that we find a way to move practicing of the Big Five up on our priority lists and spend more time in the mindset of discovery. It's hard—and the thing that mostly gets in the way is our to-do list, intensified by a good dose of urgency and stress. It is much like physical fitness: We know that if we eat well and exercise we will be calmer and more productive, yet we tend to put off these activities until we have more time and feel less stress.

We need our innovation stamina most when the circumstances of our lives are most demanding and we are tired, overworked, or burnt-out. Being in a space of discovery can help you manage and find solutions for the issues that stress you out. Ideally this means you would make time for your practice of the Big Five today, so that you can use the mindset of discovery when your schedule and life get out of balance tomorrow.

A high innovation fitness level can help us thrive in many circumstances and sustains our energy, passion—and sometimes sanity.

Barrier 3: Lack of Engagement

A lot of us work for companies that are not perfect in our eyes. On some days, we may be downright disillusioned with our company's mission or how we're treated. This might cause us to wonder why we should even bother to innovate. Is the innovation only to serve the company? Aren't the profits all going to stay at the top of the organization anyway?

Here is the thing: You get to choose where you work. Sometimes you have more flexibility, sometimes you have less. However, we all ought to innovate for ourselves *every day*, even if we feel distrust or lack of engagement at work. While it's true that our innovations may ultimately benefit—and perhaps even be owned by—our company, increasing innovation fitness and becoming a more innovative person will ultimately serve you, your family, your career (the direction of which you can't necessarily predict), your retirement, and your community. We should be innovators for the sake of a better life and a deeper contribution to the world we live in. You don't need to do a lot of research to come to the conclusion that a life lived in discovery and innovation is more interesting, more exciting, and generally happier than a stagnant one. Innovate for yourself; the results of your innovation will always help more than just your company.

Barrier 4: Politics and Internal Dynamics

Politics and territorialism can be brutal when it comes to stifling innovation initiatives and discouraging individual contributions to innovation. To be honest, I don't think I would fare very well in a highly politicized organization. As improvisers, the only politics we are involved in on stage is limited to whoever's in the White House and whichever party did the most ridiculous things that week. The game playing that often serves career jockeying and political positioning within large organizations can be tough to handle. But I've witnessed something throughout the years that may provide some assistance. When someone becomes undeniably innovative, he gains the recognition and respect of everyone around him. Suddenly the positioning—and the who's-in-whose-camp gaming—goes away, because no matter what politics are going on, *everyone* wants an innovative person on their team.

Barrier 5: Workload

There's another obstacle to innovative behavior that's actually quite simple and practical. Many times, especially in situations of understaffing, coming up with good ideas and being innovative means an increase in workload. It's easy for people to say, "That's a great idea—let us know when you get it done," "I really like how you think, you're so innovative—could you head up that initiative?" or "Wow, you work so well with others—congratulations on being named head of the committee." I get it: Sometimes there's a price for being innovative. But we have to be honest about the rewards that come with it, too—and look at the bigger picture in terms of choices we make about our careers and our lives. For me personally, the excitement and thrill of being part of a new and innovative initiative always trumps the extra work it may entail. Also, if we do a good job at the beginning of an innovative process, making sure that we ask for as much help as we can get, we can not only reduce the amount of work we have to do, we also increase innovation by increasing the size and diversity of the team.

APPLICATION EXAMPLE: JUMPING IN

Another way to describe jumping in is reducing hesitation. In improv there is no space reserved for hesitation. We simply start. Early on in my performance career I developed a simple backstage warm up, which I continue to this day, that allows me to practice eliminating hesitation and jumping in. Hesitation to me often feels like giving my brain too much time to manufacture the next idea, which is why the word *discovery* is so important to me, both as an innovator and as a performer. I believe it is much faster and almost always more interesting to get empty and then discover the next idea instead of getting serious and manufacturing the next idea.

My practice: I draw an imaginary line on the floor, which I transform into the world's most powerful vacuum. As I stride across the line, that vacuum sucks every thought out of my brain and leaves my mind completely empty. Completely empty, I simply verbalize as my foot hits the ground—or if I'm backstage, I say to myself the next thought that pops into my mind. After

(Continued)

five minutes of doing this over and over, I am much more in the mindset of discovery than in the mindset of fear or of idea manufacturing.

A more practical way of getting empty is to try to purge all of your preconceived, biased, or typical thoughts on the subject you are innovating. Write them down, get them out, and try to get as empty as possible before you discover the fresh batch of thoughts and ideas that can come from the current moment.

The goal here is to reduce the amount of time your mind has to convince you to just keep waiting. If you are busy doing, the voice of hesitation will be silenced.

Jumping In Fitness Plan and Workouts

Put on your workout clothes! We have broken down jumping in into several "muscles" you can exercise and have distilled a few tactics you can incorporate in your routine to make jumping in a breeze.

Muscles to Exercise

1. Relax and breathe.
2. Divide beginning into a series of steps and do the next small thing.
3. Think *forward*, lean in, and have your heart draw you toward what could be next.
4. Don't think of the whole project; just think of the first moment of the first step.
5. Consider the risk and opportunity cost of not jumping in.

Tactics to Practice

1. Give yourself deadlines.
2. Have other people hold you accountable for when you said you would begin.
3. Listen to your body—if it says go, just go.
4. Apply the 70 percent rule—if you are 70 percent sure about something, make a decision and adjust later.

5. Make a bold step—create a situation in which there is no turning back, only moving forward.

A few ideas to incorporate these tactics into your daily routine include creating accountability circles of people you trust whom you meet with regularly to report progress toward various goals; deciding on and sticking to your jumping in moments for the week; creating a few reasonable criteria, which you check before you go—if they are met your decision to begin is automatic; asking those around you for a gut check and then sharing yours.

Once again, the following are 10 ways you can practice jumping in outside of your daily routine:

1. Always be the first to jump into the cold lake or pool.
2. Listen to an acoustical piece of music and begin to sing words. Don't worry about the words making sense, rhyming, or even being words, just start singing.
3. The next five times that you are in a meeting and the leader asks for people to share, saying "Who wants to go first?" raise your hand immediately.
4. Find a simple, no-risk project around the house. Figure out what information is needed for you to feel comfortable about beginning the project, collect half that information, and begin anyway.
5. There is a person in your life you have wanted to reconnect with for a while. Write the letter or e-mail to them tonight!
6. Grab your kid's Legos but don't grab the directions. Build something fast; just go
7. Have someone you trust buy three types of food whose flavor you might find interesting, such as garlic, cinnamon, or something a bit spicy but not gross. Close your eyes and have her feed you a spoonful without telling you what it is.
8. If there is a chance to either sit or dance, choose dancing.
9. If someone looks as if he needs help finding something—for instance, in a store, on a bus, or in an airport—and you think

(Continued)

you can help him, approach him with a smile and ask, "Can I help you find something?"

10. Choose three things that you know you have to get done in the next 30 days. Rank them according to how much you don't want to do each one. Do the one you want to do least in the next 24 hours.

13

The Desire for Change

Mícheál

Tried to video chat with you but you did not answer.

Liam

I have not completed my profile, I am not sure if I need that in my life.

Mícheál

It's really a cool feature; you can even post videos to others in our group.

Liam

I still am using my original laptop and it doesn't have a camera.

Mícheál

No worries, it is iOS and Android enabled.

Liam

Is it flip phone enabled?

Mícheál

You could use the computer and camera in the conference room.

Liam

I tried and it asked me to set up a security code and password, so, not for me.

Mícheál

Home computer?

Liam

I am using Windows XP at home, which is no longer supported by our IT platform.

Mícheál

Computers at library?

Liam

By library, do you mean the government's data collection initiative?

Mícheál

Starbucks?

Liam

Hacker town!

Mícheál

With all that outdated technology how do you watch movies?

Liam

Easy, I even have two options.

Mícheál

What are you talking about?

Liam

I buy a lot of movies at garage sales and I can watch both kinds because I have both a VHS *and* a Betamax player in my basement!

So, thank you—sincerely. We truly are grateful that you read this book. We put a lot of time and effort into creating something that we thought could help you be your most innovative self, spend more time in the mindset of discovery, and live a deeper and more enriched life. We hope it did.

So here comes a perhaps unpleasant statement of reality: In no way, shape, or form can this book—on its own, at least—enhance your ability to innovate, increase the amount of time you spend in the mindset of discovery, or deepen and enrich your life. As a matter of fact, nothing except *you* can get that done for you.

It gets worse: It won't be easy. As a matter of fact, as with any long-term sustainable behavioral change, it will probably be quite challenging. But we believe you can do it—and hopefully something in this book has inspired you to believe that you can do it, too.

We've introduced you to our learning model, to the mindset of discovery, and to the Big Five behaviors we recommend practicing to stay more consistently in that mindset. We stated several times that practicing is absolutely the most essential part of the program. We also talked about the conditions that should be in place while you're practicing: to be comfortable being uncomfortable and to be of service to others. Those are both important and necessary to make the practice potent enough to affect long-term behavior change.

So as you end your time with this book—and hopefully begin your time with your innovation fitness plan and practice regimen—it seems appropriate to talk about the third condition of practice, which truly is the first step in all of this. It is the honest, authentic, and personal *desire to change*. If the desire to change isn't there at the beginning of your journey, you may end up spinning your wheels, going off on tangents, and wondering why changes in your behaviors aren't showing up.

I have struggled with this condition and this desire to change many times in my innovation journey and hundreds of times in other aspects of my life. But what is clear after 49 years of life, 22 years of improvisation, and 15 years of trying to spend most of my time in the mindset of discovery is that without a true desire for change, I simply won't be able to drastically improve, alter who I am for the better, and create habitual and sustainable behaviors and mindsets in my life.

I would like to share two examples of this condition in my life—one of success and one that I'm still trying to accomplish. Let's tackle the hard thing—the one that I have struggled with for years—first.

In 1984 I reported to football camp at St. Norbert College in De Pere, Wisconsin. I was excited that the coach had invited me to come in early as a freshman. I was looking forward to playing a game I loved and had been playing since third grade at this higher level of competition. The first few days were tough: two practices per day in the August heat, weightlifting, and running in between. But it was also tough emotionally; not only wasn't I one of the most talented guys on the team, I was very worried about even making the 48-man roster. This was a group of football players that was faster, stronger, and harder hitting than I had ever experienced. I was truly in another league.

So after the first week I had a difficult conversation with the coaches. They respected my effort, they loved my positive attitude, and I seemed to have found a soft spot in their hearts. They wanted me on the team, but I wasn't good enough at my current position so they suggested I try moving to the nose guard/tackle position. The new position would allow me to make the most out of my toughness and persistence without necessarily needing the speed and strength that my former position required. I would, however, be expected to gain weight, as I was simply too light to hold my ground as a nose guard.

I made the team. I played football at St. Norbert College all the way through my senior year. And I went from 200 pounds to 250 pounds in four months. When I came home for Christmas break many of my high school friends didn't recognize me. I sustained that weight throughout college—although I was in pretty good shape because of the combination of the exercise I was getting on the football team and pure and sweet youthful metabolism.

After college, football ended—and so did the exercise. Working and playing hard seemed to leave no time for a regimen of fitness. Ten years after reporting to my first college football practice I was 250 pounds and not sporting an athletic physique.

Now, at age 49, I still weigh over an eighth of a ton (250 lbs.). My weight has gone up and down, and I have lost and gained more than 50 pounds five times since college. I have tried lots of ways to maintain my weight and fitness, but in the end, I really don't think I have been able to find my sincere and real desire to change. And each year I age, the tougher it gets.

However, there's a different area of my life in which I have been able to find consistency, sustainability, and long-term behavioral change. While writing this book, I will be celebrating my twentieth year of sobriety. It became clear in 1995 that my love of Guinness and Irish whiskey had grown into a problem and was creating circumstances that were clearly outside of my values and my priorities in life. Most importantly, my drinking was getting in the way of the most important thing in my life: my relationship with my then-girlfriend Jenni Lilledahl. With good help, support, and guidance, I was able to start my journey of sobriety on the right foot. I took it day by day and did the simple and small things it took to maintain and build upon each step and upon each new chapter of this new set of behaviors and life.

I have done a good job with my sobriety: I have kept it top of mind; created small and more elaborate processes to make it habitual; and embraced a lifelong, slow, and sometimes hard path. I have found support systems and mentors, I practice each day, and I strive to continue to learn and gain more understanding and wisdom to keep me on the straight and narrow.

The results of my work and practice have produced amazing and miraculous benefits and results. My personal and business lives have grown and been strengthened as a direct result of my sobriety mindset. The biggest manifestation of this life change is my relationship and marriage of 17 years with Jenni, the same person that my drinking almost made me lose forever. Change can happen, behaviors can lead to mindsets, and mindsets can become sustainable.

I share both of these examples with you not because they are unique or spectacular—but because I want you to know that everyone struggles and succeeds in different parts of life. I, too, need to continue to find ways to find the condition of real desire for change.

Throughout this book, both you and our whole writing team have been fortunate to hear wonderful examples, inspirations, wisdom, and tools from all of the amazing people I had the honor and privilege to interview. We have placed their interviews to help you hear and see and understand the underlying point in that chapter of the book—and what it looks like in the reality of that person's life.

For this discussion about finding the courage to have a real desire to change, no one lives it or says it better than our dear Miss Wanda from Dexter Avenue King Memorial Baptist Church:

John: I'm aware that I come from a privileged white background; I've never had to live in a place of fear because of the color of my skin or where I'm from. But I'm also interested in the fact that obviously things weren't perfect after Selma and after 1965, and to this day. I know that just blocks away from where you give your tour there are still police at the civil rights memorial because of bomb threats.

I know you live in a world where people are judgmental. When I talk about fear, I talk about relatively silly fears of sharing ideas and things that happen in the workplace. But you've lived real fear before—and I wonder how you've been able to manage to live a life of service in the face of this fear?

Did your mother leave you with any wisdom on this? Did she talk about what to do when it gets to a point that someone might even harm you—yet you still have to try not to be affected by the fear?

Wanda: Absolutely. I've learned that if you are fighting for a cause that you truly believe is just and right, it's worth it. I truly believe, and I understand better now, that the Montgomery bus boycott and the civil rights movement were both based on the fact that not just one or two people, but a whole society of black people, had gotten tired of living under the injustices. So whatever the consequences were, it was going to be worth it.

I had a situation in Atlanta some years ago, when a man walked up to me when I was standing at a bus stop and put a knife to my throat. He grabbed my arm and was pulling me down the street, telling me I was going with him.

I yanked my arm back and walked back to the stop where at least 10 people were standing. And I told him, I said, "I don't know you. I'm not going with you." He put the knife back up to my throat and he said, "I could slit your throat." And I said, "Well, you go right ahead." There was something inside of me. Outside of that moment, I never would've known or thought that I would have ever said and been that assured, even if he had hurt me. But I was so determined, and thought, "I don't care what you say, I'm not going with you."

I was angrier with the 10 people standing there watching who did nothing than I was with the man who put the knife to my throat.

John: Do you think they were just scared? Is that why they didn't do something?

Wanda: Yes. And when you look at the civil rights movement, you see much of the same thing. Countless people wouldn't join the movement—attend the marches and protests—because they were afraid. There were enough others who were courageous enough—and determined enough to see change come—to be willing to step forward. Enough people stepped forward in the moment and over the years to make it very effective. And it did make a difference. It made a change.

John: As you look back, and maybe think of the sacrifice and fear people such as your mother had to undergo—and I know there's lots and lots of work still to be done and it's anything but perfect—but does it feel as if it was worth it? Do people think it was worth it?

Wanda: That's another thing I say on the tour. I say, "Here we are. Standing in the basement of Dexter Avenue King Memorial Baptist Church where 50, 60 years ago, it was unlawful for people of many ethnicities, black people and white people, to be here together." I say, "Here we are. Now we can ride the bus, we can drink from any fountain, we can go to any restaurant we want to." I say, "We have inherited many freedoms because many people marched, did sit-ins, and protested until the laws were changed. And now we're the inheritors of these freedoms."

But I still remind everybody on the tour that the work isn't done. It continues, because freedom work is a work of love against evil. Every day, all of us are confronted with making that decision. Will I love instead of being hateful? Because all racism is to me, is one of those categories that people use to say, "I don't want to like you. I hate you."

But I say you can flip that same coin and come up with many reasons why I love you instead. So let us be the agents of love rather than hate.

John: And that's back to your intentional choice, right?

Wanda: Yes. It starts with self.

It certainly does, Miss Wanda. Thank you for showing us all what that intentional choice of one's self can look like.

I would like to end our time together with a small exercise and then some thoughts on the topic of hope.

The exercise is a simple one. It comes from improvisation and is something you have done a million times as a child. I want you to pretend. Pretend that it is five years from now and that you have undergone a transformation—that you are a slightly different version of the you that you are today. Imagine yourself as a more nimble, more open-minded you. Pretend that you are better at taking risks and thinking differently, that you are a fierce and friendly collaborator and ensemble member. Pretend that ideas flow from you with ease, that you have lost your fear of ambiguity, that you have turned the things you perceive today as obstacles in your life into opportunities. Perhaps this new version of you is a great listener who makes very few judgments. The future you jumps right into things and communicates your point of view in a clear and authentic voice and naturally reframes new information and circumstances that come your way. Pretend that the new you is innovative in everything you do.

Now that you have this version of what you might be like from this exercise, pretend to put this newly found version of you in situations that you commonly face in your business and personal life. How does this version of you react? What different choices do you make? What new outcomes are created by this version of you?

The goal of this book was to give you some small bits of information, a few parts of a plan, and some examples of how you can become the version of you that you just imagined.

And so we end with hope.

Our sincere and deep hope is that you begin—or if you have begun, that you continue to work toward—being your most innovative self.

Our hope is that you will define innovation as how you behave and the mindset you live in. Our hope is that you will create a practice plan that allows you to create sustainability in your innovation. Our hope is that you will become your most innovative self, and that you will have a life that is filled with rewarding work, meaningful relationships, and a sense of service to others. That is our hope for you and for us and for all.

Be sure to laugh today.

References

Accountemps. October 24, 2012. "Workplace Frights." News release. http://accountemps
.rhi.mediaroom.com/workplace-fears.

Adolphs, Ralph. 2015. Interview by Lulu Miller and Alix Spiegel on "Fearless," from NPR's
Invisibilia series, January 16, 2015. www.npr.org/programs/invisibilia/377515477/
fearless.

Anderson, Jeffrey, Jared Nielsen, Brandon Zielinski, Michael Ferguson, and Janet Lainhart.
2013. "An Evaluation of the Left-Brain vs. Right-Brain Hypothesis with Resting State
Functional Connectivity Magnetic Resonance Imaging." *PLOS ONE* 8(8): e71275.
doi:10.1371/journal.pone.0071275.

Anderson, Norman B., et al. 2014. *Stress in America™: Are Teens Adopting Adults' Stress
Habits?* Survey report. Washington DC: American Psychological Association, February 11.

APA Center for Organizational Excellence. 2014. *2014 Work and Well-Being Survey.* American Psychological Association, April.

Boroush, Mark. 2010. "NSF Releases New Statistics on Business Innovation." National
Science Foundation InfoBrief NSF 11-300, October. www.nsf.gov/statistics/infbrief/
nsf11300/.

Dean, Jeremy. 2013. *Making Habits, Breaking Habits.* Boston: Da Capo Press.

Dennis, Rea. 2014. "Improvised Performance: Nurturing Natural Leadership." *Journal of
Organisational Transformation and Social Change* 11(2): 108–124.

Desbordes, Gaëlle, Lobsang T. Negi, Thaddeus W. W. Pace, B. Alan Wallace, Charles L.
Raison, and Eric L. Schwartz. 2012. "Effects of Mindful-Attention and Compassion Meditation Training on Amygdala Response to Emotional Stimuli in
an Ordinary, Non-Meditative State." *Frontiers in Human Neuroscience* 6: 292.
doi:10.3389/fnhum.2012.00292.

Downey, Greg. 2015. Interview by Lulu Miller on "Fearless," from NPR's *Invisibilia* series,
January 16, 2015. www.npr.org/programs/invisibilia/377515477/fearless.

187

Duhigg, Charles. 2012. *The Power of Habit*. New York: Random House.

Dweck, Carol. 2008. *Mindset: The New Psychology of Success*. New York: Ballantine Books.

———. 2013. "Teaching a Growth Mindset." Video. "Young Minds 2013." Sydney, Australia. www.youtube.com/watch?v=kXhbtCcmsyQ.

———. n.d. "How Can you Change from a Fixed Mindset to a Growth Mindset?" http://mindsetonline.com/changeyourmindset/firststeps/index.html. Accessed July 11, 2014.

Eisenberger, Naomi, Matthew Lieberman, and Kipling Williams. 2003. "Does Rejection Hurt? An fMRI Study of Social Exclusion." *Science* 302 (5643, October 10): 290–292.

Eurostat and Organisation for Economic Co-Operation and Development (OECD). 2005. *Oslo Manual: Guidelines for Collecting and Interpreting Innovation Data*. 3rd. ed. Paris: OECD Publications, 46.

Gigerenzer, Gerd. 2014. Interview by Justin Fox. "Instinct Can Beat Analytical Thinking." *Harvard Business Review*, June 20.

Gino, Francesca, Alison Brooks, and Maurice Schweitzer. 2012. "Anxiety, Advice, and the Ability to Discern: Feeling Anxious Motivates." *Journal of Personality and Social Psychology* 102 (3): 497–512. doi: 10.1037/a0026413.

Goldsmith, Marshall. 2014. "When Fear and Learning Collide." *Talent Management*, June 20.

Govindarajan, Vijay, and Chris Trimble. 2010. *The Other Side of Innovation: Solving the Execution Challenge*. Boston: Harvard Business Press.

Hewlett, Sylvia Ann, Melinda Marshall, Laura Sherbin, and Tara Gonsalves. 2013. *Innovation, Diversity and Market Growth*. New York: Center for Talent Innovation.

Imaretska, Elena, and John Sweeney. 2015. "Creating an Innovation Fitness Plan." *Chief Learning Officer*, January 21: 18–21.

Jung, Rex. 2013. Interview by Krista Tippett. *Creativity and the Everyday Brain*, May 2 http://www.onbeing.org/program/creativity-and-everyday-brain/1879.

Jung, Rex, Brittany Mead, Jessica Carrasco, and Ranee Flores. 2013. "The Structure of Creative Cognition in the Human Brain." *Frontiers in Human Neuroscience* 7. doi:10.3389/fnhum.2013.00330.

Limb, C. J., and A. R. Braun. 2008. "Neural Substrates of Spontaneous Musical Performance: An FMRI Study of Jazz Improvisation." *PLOS ONE* 3 (2): e1679. doi:10.1371/journal.pone.0001679.

Liu, Siyuan, et al. 2012. "Neural Correlates of Lyrical Improvisation: An fMRI Study of Freestyle Rap." *Scientific Reports* 2. doi:10.1038/srep00834.

McGonigal, Kelly. 2015. Interview by Tom Crain http://www.mprnews.org/story/2015/05/28/bcst-books-thread-stress. *"The Upside of Stress:" How Stress Can Actually Be Healthy*, May 28.

Milliken, Francis J, Elizabeth W. Morrison, and Patricia F Hewlin. 2003. "An Exploratory Study of Employee Silence: Issues That Employees Don't Communicate Upward and Why." *Journal of Management Studies* 40 (6): 1453–1476. doi: 10.111/1467-6486.00387.

Morrison, Elizabeth W., and Frances J. Milliken. 2000. "Organizational Silence: A Barrier to Change and Development in a Pluralistic World." *The Academy of Management Review* 25 (4): 706–725.

Piurek, Ryan. 2008. "Stressing Out, Outing Stress." *Indiana University Research and Creative Activity* 30 (2).

Sawyer, Keith. 2007. *Group Genius: the Creative Power of Collaboration*. New York: Basic Books.

Sawyer, Keith, and Stacy Dezutter. 2009. "Distributed Creativity: How Collective Creations Emerge from Collaboration." *Psychology of Aesthetics, Creativity and the Arts* 3 (2): 81–92.

Scholz, Jan, Miriam C. Klein, Timothy E. J. Behrens, and Heidi Johansen-Berg. 2009. "Training Induces Changes in White-Matter Architecture." *Nature Neuroscience* 12:1370–1371.

Wellman, Cara, Sarah Brown, and Shannon Henning. 2005. "Mild, Short-Term Stress Alters Dendritic Morphology in Rat Medial Prefrontal Cortex." *Cerebral Cortex* 15:1714–1722.

Yeager, David Scott, and Carol Dweck. 2012. "Mindsets That Promote Resilience: When Students Believe That Personal Characteristics Can Be Developed." *Educational Psychologist* 47 (4): 302–314.

Index

191